The Professional
Woman's Guide to finding 30
guilt-free hours a month

KATE CHRISTIE

Me Time

The Professional Woman's Guide to finding 30 guilt-free hours a month

---

Proudly self-published in Australia by Kate Christie in 2014

Second edition

info@timestylers.com.au

www.timestylers.com.au

www.babysittersandmore.com.au

ISBN: 978-0-992-57920-3

Editor: Robert Watson

Cover and Internal Design: Pipeline Design (pipelinedesign.com.au)

Cover Photography: Shutterstock (shutterstock.com)

Printed in Australia by Minuteman Press Prahran 63034

To my beautiful family
Daniel, Freddie, Wally, Peggy, Bobbo and Janey x

ACKNOWLEDGEMENTS

Thank you

Thank you to everyone who generously provided support and guidance while I was writing *Me Time*.

To my clients and friends, for your input – particularly the clever, wonderful, talented women in my world who helped road test *Me Time*.

Special thanks to the inspirational Natasha Stott Despoja, Janine Allis, Carolyn Creswell, Holly Kramer, Amy Poynton, Nicola Moras, Megan Della-Camina, Angela Counsel, Christie Nicholas, Ruth MacKay, Anoushka Gungadin, Fatima Dib, Sarah Wood, Renee Ackary and Tanya McVicar for generously giving your time to be interviewed about your own experiences.

Special thanks to Laurie Wood of HRascent who saw my vision for *Me Time* and provided valuable support and sponsorship. And to my very clever best friend Tan, a successful business woman and mum.

To my mum and dad who have always been my biggest supporters in absolutely everything I do. And most of all, to my family Daniel, Freddie, Wally and Peggy who gave me the space, time, motivation, love and encouragement to realise my dream of writing this book.

Kate x

What would 30 extra hours a month mean to you?

30 hours of quality time for yourself; 30 hours of quality time with your family; 30 hours of quality time to grow your success - greater health, greater wealth and greater happiness. Can you even put a dollar figure on that?

Let's try:

30 hours of quality time with your family	=	*PRICELESS*
30 hours of quality time to spend on yourself	=	*PRICELESS*
30 hours of quality time to grow your success (say you earn $70 an hour)	=	*$25,200 a year*

Now let's get started!

CONTENTS

HOW TO USE THIS BOOK

This book, *Me Time*, contains a lot of information. It also contains a number of exercises and actions for you to complete, all designed with the ultimate goal of getting you back 30 hours a month to live the life you want.

The exercises and actions are set out in easy steps, however they will challenge you to reveal your underlying drivers and desires in life. It is critical that you complete each and every exercise. Why? Because this is where your brain takes the printed words in *Me Time* and transfers them into your real-time world. Only you can do this. Your home life, your work life, your family life, your personal interests, and the language you use are all unique to you. Besides, the exercises are where the gold is buried. Getting time back will take a bit of work - but if you don't dig a little then you won't find the nuggets.

The exercises and actions can either be completed in your copy of *Me Time* or you can download the *Me Time* Workbook for free from www.timestylers.com.au (every time you see this icon, it's a reminder to use the *Me Time* Workbook). The act of hand writing your answers in the *Me Time* Workbook will make for a deeper, more considered, and more successful way to digest the information in *Me Time*. Plus, that keeps your copy of *Me Time* nice and pristine.

Even though *Me Time* is targeted at busy professional women and business owners who are also mums, the techniques covered in the *5 Steps to Being SMART* can be used by women and men without kids and by working dads.

Just because you don't have kids does not mean that your daily trip to the supermarket on the way home from work is the best use of your time!

IT'S A BIRD! IT'S A PLANE! NO - IT'S SUPERWOMAN!

What do you think of her? You know who I mean. She is poised, relaxed, in complete control of her successful business or career, all without compromising her home life. She has more freedom than you. She has more balance than you. She has more energy, less guilt, less stress, and greater happiness. She truly seems to *have it all*. She is unfazed, unruffled and, quite frankly, unbelievable.

Have you ever wondered how the hell she does it? It's simple. Under that lovely suit she is wearing is a figure-hugging, red lycra cat suit with a large *S* emblazoned across her magnificent bosom.

Just kidding. She isn't actually Superwoman. She's not even a *super woman*. She is just like you. The only difference is that she is a whole lot smarter when it comes to managing her time.

When someone asks you, *How are you?* do you respond, *I'm busy?* Yes, you do. But when was the last time you said, *I'm great! Work is flying and I have the freedom and balance I need to live a healthy and fulfilling lifestyle. I am living the dream!* Never?

I am a self-proclaimed high achiever and recovered sufferer of superwoman-ness. I am one of a generation of clever women who was told that we could have it all. And I truly believed it. And for a long time it worked - I was used to getting exactly what I wanted through sheer hard work. I too wore a lycra cat suit under my shirt with *S* emblazoned across my less substantial bosom. I simply flew up that career ladder with my fist clenched ready to smash through the glass ceiling.

Hard Work = Success = Having It All = the simple formula by which I lived my life

Then, in quick succession I had three babies all while trying to maintain my career, juggle work, a husband and a home. For five years straight my poor body was either pregnant or breast feeding or both. I was frazzled, exhausted and working like a crazy woman trying to be the *best* of everything to everyone. Best career girl, best mum, best wife, best home maker... something had to give.

Clearly, it was time to rethink the formula.

At the time I knew a few Superwomen who seemed to have it all with the minimum of fuss. What were they doing that I was not? What were they doing that I could not?

How the hell did *they* do it all?

It took me a while, but eventually I realised that I had confused having it all with doing it all. I might be clever, but I sure wasn't being smart. And that was my big mistake. What I realised through my own journey from here to insanity and back, boils down to this:

Having It All does not mean *Doing It All*

And you? You are a clever, savvy, successful woman. But are you being *smart*?

You have a lot of balls in the air and mostly you are happy to let a few drop here and there - but as you progress in your career or as your business grows, it seems that those balls are multiplying exponentially. It's getting harder to keep the balls in the air and the challenge you face is that you may well drop the lot.

You have achieved your success with talent and hard work. But these qualities won't take you to the next stage. You need to start doing things differently. Your current approach in trying to *do it all* represents the biggest risk to your success. And frankly, you are bleeding time.

Me Time will help you reorganise your time effectively, bringing success at home and work to you quicker. You got yourself this far, all you need are some new systems to help you maintain what you are *time managing* well, discard your *time wasters*, and some new Tools and support to enhance and sustain your performance.

I am going to coach you on how to manage your time on the home front the SMART way - let's work on getting you back 30 hours a month to live the life you want*.

It's time to live SMART!

All About Alice

I'd like to introduce you to Alice - your companion on this journey to getting back 30 hours a month to live the life you want. You will be able to read over Alice's shoulder as she works her way through *Me Time* and completes the exercises and actions to get back her own 30 hours a month. My intention is that you will draw inspiration from Alice's progress, along with a few ideas on what you can do differently for yourself. Alice is your Case Study, but also a little lifebuoy that you can cling to when you feel like you might be going under.

The wonderful thing about Alice is that she calls it as she sees it. While you might try and fudge the data in the exercises you are asked to complete, you can rest assured that Alice will be airing all her dirty laundry. With any luck this will encourage you to give yourself permission to let your guard down. If Alice can let it all hang out then so can you. Remember - no-one is reading over your shoulder or judging you.

You may not love Alice - she can be a bit cheeky and self-deprecating, but she's your guide, not your friend. Despite this, you might see a bit of yourself in Alice so feel free to laugh at her (after all, you will just be laughing at yourself).

Alice isn't a real person, she is an amalgamation of a lot of different women I know.

---

*The *5 Steps to Being SMART* is a process to optimise your results - you still need to do the work. If you invest the time you will get back hours of lost time. Don't dabble or go in half-hearted. Don't pull out halfway through. Don't drop the ball. If you want to get back 30 hours a month it's up to you to put in. However if you are a person who really needs personal coaching to make it all happen, my contact details are shown in Part Four.

PART 1
IT'S TIME!

ALL ABOUT YOU

Alice's Me Time Diary

I am Alice. 38 years old. Senior Associate knocking on the door of Partnership with a big Consultancy firm. 2 children, Henry aged 11 and Olive aged 9.

Happily married, mostly, to John (who sometimes masquerades as my third child).

We have a healthy combined income, live in a beautiful house in our suburb of choice, 2 cars, a gym membership that I don't use, a dog, a cat, not enough time with the kids and no time for each other.

At work I am held up as a role model and mentor for the young female talent that the Partnership is terrified of losing. See, they say to the young female recruits as they point to me, you CAN have it all - a successful career, a beautiful family, and all the trappings of success - just look at Alice. Smile Alice. Smile.

If only they knew.

In reality I am literally just holding it together. I work full time in a well-paid job that I love. I also work an infinite number of hours a week for no money at all as a mum (a job I also love, I just wish it paid more). I am all things to all people - mum, cook, cleaner, washer woman, shopper, taxi driver, teacher, nurse, counsellor, basketball coach (don't ask), football team manager (don't ask), wife, lover, accountant, advisor, mentor, manager, friend, daughter, sister . . .

Multi-task is my middle name. I can read an email while making the school lunches. I am adept at dropping into the supermarket each day and grabbing just what we need for that night and not a bean more, mobile pressed to my ear with one hand, pushing the trolley with the other, while steering with my hip. No-one can run faster in heels than me when it comes to dashing for my car to get from the city to the kids at school, while making a mental To Do List of everything I need to do tonight, tomorrow and the next day. I am a whirlwind as I vacuum the floor, feed the pets, make dinner for the family, help with homework, listen to John's day and then collapse into bed.

Awesome. Just awesome. Congratulations Alice my girl - you are living the dream! Not.

I am being pulled in so many different directions that I fear one day my arms, legs and head will simply pop off and my torso will be set upon by all those who want a piece of me.

Sure, I might look like I have it all. I sure as hell do it all. But enough is enough.

Despite appearances, I don't have it all. I don't even want it all. I certainly no longer want to do it all. I am calling it for what it is: My name is Alice and I need help.

Please.

◇◇

I know you

I know you. While you have all the appearance of absolute success in everything you do, scratch below the surface and the reality is that you are panicking, even just a little.

Most time-poor successful women who are also mums live with a constant undercurrent of stress and guilt. However, consistent with buying into the superwoman myth, they think they need to do it all. And so they don't change. Or, if they do try to change, they generally make unrealistic and unsustainable promises to themselves and, like embarking on a crash diet, they quickly fall back to old habits and feel worse for the failed attempt.

> ***92% of the women I ask tell me that they want more time.***

It's OK. You aren't alone.

Women are sick of the constant juggle. They have confused having it all with doing it all and have forgotten that having it all really just means having access to all the bits that are important to them. Throughout *Me Time* you will hear from women I interviewed for their insights on how they manage their time. I hope their advice and learnings resonate with you and that you draw inspiration from them.

So, when was the last time you just stopped and enjoyed the moment? Or did something for yourself that didn't involve work, favours for others or your family? Or looked forward to going out instead of falling into bed exhausted? Or didn't beat yourself up for your choices?

You have lost sight of what's important to you. You have all these amazing balls in the air and yet you have no time to enjoy any of them because you are juggling your arms off to make sure you don't actually drop one.

Hell yes, you are damned clever and successful. But lady, that does not make you smart.

I was you

The reason why I know you and why I know that I can help you, is that I was you. You can read more about me at the end of *Me Time* in About Kate.

For me, in trying to do it all I lost sight of what was most important to me. I did not set appropriate boundaries (like don't take work calls when you are on reading duty at school) and so I never lived in the moment either at home or at work. If I was at work I would be feeling guilty about not being with my children. If I was with my children I would spend half my time thinking about work. Regardless of what I was actually supposed to be doing at any given time, my mind was elsewhere or in many places, forever making mental lists. I was constantly available to everyone. I was never available to just myself. I was highly stressed. I was terribly guilty. And I felt I could not be successful at work and at home at the same time.

Sound familiar?

As a solutions-oriented person, I set about looking for a book with all the answers to how I could better live my life. However, the books I found were either full of theory and psychology or fluff and nonsense and frankly took up too much of my already over-stretched, precious time just in the reading.

And so, not satisfied with what was available I redesigned my time myself. I developed a simple *Do It Myself* process that helped me track and rate my time; analyse what my time management habits were costing me; and then implemented a series of simple and sustainable solutions to manage my time smarter.

I broke my process into 5 distinct steps and I now mentor other clever, successful women to help them work through and implement the *5 Steps to Being SMART.*

My promises to you

I want you to read *Me Time,* absorb the underlying messages, undertake the exercises and take action to get back 30 hours a month. I want you to start living the life you want.

In return, here are my promises to you:

- The *5 Steps to Being SMART* worked for me and are now available to work for you. If you are ready to take action, *Me Time* will help you succeed.
- *Me Time* provides the process to help you identify lost time, implement new habits to find 30 hours a month, and then track and sustain your success.
- You will be left with simple, smart and sustainable solutions which will give you back hours of quality time to live the life you want.
- I don't do fluff and nonsense. I know you are busy and that you want to hear it straight. I respect your time too much to stuff you around.
- *Me Time* is specifically targeted at clever, successful women who are also mums. You will work out what's most important to you and quantify the cost of what's not important, all supported by techniques and tools you can adapt to your unique situation.

The mistakes we make ... again and again

Managing your time better is not about being perfect. It's about being smarter. Without making mistakes we would have nothing to learn from or to improve on. However - and this is a big however - sometimes we don't learn from our mistakes. Sometimes we fall into the nasty little habit of repeating the same mistakes over and over.

And worse, some of the mistakes we continually repeat exacerbate our major pain points - such as not having enough time. Some of our behaviours actually result in us having even less time. *Yes*, we can be our own worst enemy.

There are some consistent themes when it comes to mistakes around time management. Have a look at the following 7 most common mistakes busy, clever women make when it comes to managing their time well, and see how you line up with them. By working through the *5 Steps to Being SMART*, and identifying your own behaviours, you will be able to avoid making these mistakes:

---

1. You compare yourself to other women

You look at what other women around you are doing. To you, many of these women appear to be superwomen. They do it all and they have it all. They are perfect and you are not.

Stop!

Stop comparing yourself to other women. Stop thinking they are doing a better job than you. Stop second guessing your own actions based on your perception of how someone else lives her life.

Many of the women you are comparing yourself with are full of the same self-doubt as they look at you and wonder how you do it all. Ironic, yes?

Stop chasing her dreams.

Set your own goals. Identify your own Values. Live your own life and do it a whole lot smarter and with greater happiness and confidence than you are right now.

Overcoming Mistake 1 will be addressed in Step 1 Self Aware.

2. You were told you could have it all. So, what happened?

You might think that you can have it all. You might even think you need it all. Wrong. It's time to think about what you really want. You don't actually need to have it all - you only need to aim to have all the bits that are important to you.

You have set the bar too high. Focus on what's most important and forget the rest - it's just a distraction.

Think about it as being the best version of you.

Overcoming Mistake 2 is what *Me Time* is all about!

3. You don't know where your time goes

You feel busy. You tell other people that you are busy. You certainly have all the appearance of being busy. But just what is it you are actually doing each day that has generated all of this busy-ness?

If you don't know, in detail, where you are spending your time each day, then you can't know what changes you can make to free up your time.

Stop the busy-ness and take some time to think this through.

Overcoming Mistake 3 is addressed in Step 2 Map.

4. You don't say No

If you are continually saying *Yes* to all of the requests that come your way (from your colleagues, children, partner, friends and family) then two things will happen:

- you will quickly run out of time; and
- the requests for help will keep coming in, as you are renowned in your circle as the Go To girl who always says Yes and who always delivers.

There just aren't enough hours in the day to do everything, and to be everything, for everyone. Saying *No* can be hard for a Yes-person. Like changing any habit, learning to say No is challenging and will take persistence.

Overcoming Mistake 4 is addressed later in Part One and throughout *Me Time*.

5. You don't ask for help

Not asking for help when it's needed goes hand in hand with being a Yes-person. It's a double affliction - always saying Yes to everyone else but never asking for a return favour when you need it.

Trying to do it all by yourself while attempting to maintain and grow your success is not sustainable.

Your physical and mental health and happiness could be impacted. Your relationships could be impacted. Your sense of self-worth could be impacted. Your productivity and successful career or business could be impacted.

These are significant risks.

Look at this through a different lens - if you do get to the point of burn out, in your absence you will be replaced by a team of people who will manage the many facets of your life until you get better. So, if it takes a team of people to replace you, how is it that you thought you could manage to do it all on your own?

It's OK to ask for help. It's OK to expect help. It's OK to pay for help. Start seeking help when you need it.

Overcoming Mistake 5 is addressed in Step 4 Reframe.

6. You don't schedule time for yourself

When you suddenly find yourself with a little bit of spare time, you don't spend any of that time on yourself.

The whole point of working through the *5 Steps to Being SMART* is to get you back 30 hours a month to live the life you want.

This will work. Don't forget to lock in time for yourself.

Overcoming Mistake 6 is addressed in Step 4 Reframe.

7. You don't know where to start and so you don't

You know you need to manage your time smarter, but you have 1000 excuses as to why today is not the best day to start. Today you are too busy, too tired, too unmotivated. Whatever.

There is never going to be a best day to start managing your time smarter. But you do need to pick a day. I know you are busy, so assuming you allow yourself two weeks to read *Me Time* and to complete all of the exercises, you can confidently circle a Monday at 10am three weeks from now with the entry *Start managing my time SMARTER today!*

Find the space to reframe - if you don't commit and circle a date in your diary to get started, you will put this off forever.

Overcoming Mistake 7 is addressed in Step 5 Take Control.

Some or all of these 7 mistakes will have resonated with you, so next time you catch yourself walking along the path of darkness just pause, rethink what you are doing, and change your course.

Sorry, it's a ***No*** from me ...

Alice's Me Time Diary

I hate those awkward conversations where someone is clearly building up to ask me for a favour. I feel that awkwardness to my core. And so, taking saying Yes to an art form hitherto unknown to man, I take away my discomfort by anticipating what I think the favour is going to be and I offer up my help WITHOUT EVEN BEING ASKED!

Yep.

I'm pretty sure that half the time I anticipate wrong, that whoever I am talking to is simply blowing off steam about how busy they are. And yet, the offer is already out there just begging to be accepted.

For me, it's not just that I can't say No, it's that I can't keep my mouth shut full stop!

Like today, Jules called me, stressed out about how busy she is and that she is down for scoring this weekend at the kids' basketball and that she might be stuck and ...

And ... in I jumped. Before my brain had a chance to catch up to my mouth, I said 'I can score for you'.

Why? Why? Why?

I do this ALL the time. What is this crazy need to please? To be liked? Is it a perverse desire to pretend I have lots of free time? Because I don't. Have lots of time that is.

Whatever the underlying root cause of this craziness, it is definitely crazy. Because I am a busy person, and here I am taking on more, without even being asked.

And then I got stressed. And then John cracked it with me, telling me I shouldn't take on so much and that I am already over-committed and that Jules can do her own bloody scoring and blah, blah, blah. And while he was right I certainly wasn't going to admit that to him. So I turned up the hand in the ubiquitous 'Stop Sign' and tried to tune out. Blah, blah, blah.

And of course we had an argument.

So here I am - taking on too much, offering up my precious time, getting stressed, getting angry and having an argument. About basketball scoring. Give me a break.

◊◊

Turning someone down can be confronting. Here are some ways you can politely say *No* (or at least not say *Yes*):

- Hear the person out before you jump in with an offer. They might just be letting off steam or about to tell you they need to reschedule something you had planned. Hold your tongue and let them finish.
- If they do ask for a favour which you don't really want to give, tell the truth. Try: *I'm sorry but I can't score the basketball on Saturday because I just want to watch my son play.*
- Offer an alternative that works well for you both: *I think I am on scoring the following week. Do you want to swap?*
- Don't feel the need to be a people pleaser. People are not going to like you any less if you say No to a request. Go back to the second dot point above and just tell the truth - they will actually appreciate your honesty.
- Solving problems does not mean taking on endless amounts of work. It means prioritising and delegating.

I want you to practise these responses:

- No, that won't work for me today.
- No, sorry, I am prioritising my time differently and I can't fit that in.
- No thank you, but no.
- No. Definitely not.
- No.

Very good.

— *What other women say* —

Janine Allis, Founder and Managing Director
Boost Juice (Retail Zoo)

I have a filter for the requests I receive: (i) does it interest me? (ii) can I add value? (iii) will I be able to give my best? (iv) does it fit with my family?

Holly Kramer, CEO Best & Less

You have to accept that everyone is going to want more from you – your team, your staff, your kids, your husband. You need to accept that state, find the right balance and learn to say No. What I eventually realised was that when I was over committed I did things badly, which helped no one. Now I only sign on to something if I have the time to do it properly.

Carolyn Creswell, Founder Carman's

Think of it this way – if someone came up and asked for $20 you would say No. But when they ask for your time, you say Yes. Your time is money. Say yes to the important stuff, not to everything that comes your way.

Megan Dalla-Camina, Strategist and Author of Getting Real About Having It All

I used to be a complete stress head. My stress came from never saying No *and from wanting to do too much. A lot of women I know are stressed simply for this reason. But we need to realise that we are busy with what we said* Yes *to, and when we say* Yes *to someone else we need to make sure we are not saying* No *to ourselves. Setting boundaries and learning to say* No *is incredibly important to our wellbeing, productivity and happiness.*

IT'S TIME TO PUT YOUR MONEY WHERE YOUR MOUTH IS

Alice's Me Time Diary

Staring vacantly out the window again. Mind blank. Focus lady, there is work to be done! I need a coffee before I write this report. I'll make it in the office kitchen one floor up so that I have to walk up and down the stairs. Exercise right? Plus I need to tidy my desk because I can't stand working in clutter. Check my emails. I need to get on to that report. But, first, I need to fill my water bottle. Come on Alice - FOCUS girl.

Procrastinating so effectively that there is every chance I might implode. Imagine that. Poof - she just blew up Your Honour.

C'mon! Report time.

What is SMART?

Poor time management habits are universal - procrastination, failure to plan, lack of focus, inability to delegate, not setting boundaries, never saying No, and the list goes on. Hell, if you are looking to waste a little more time before really getting stuck into *Me Time*, feel free to ponder on this some more and add your own examples of poor time management in the margin, along with a couple of doodles.

The 5 Steps to Being *SMART* outlined in Part Two of *Me Time* will take you through a series of logical exercises to gather the data on your personal poor time management habits and apply your own critical analysis to these, with a view to reframing your time to leave you with 30 (or more) reclaimed hours a month.

Sounds easy, right? Well, no. If it was that easy you would have reframed your time already.

The *5 Steps to Being SMART* is not a slapdash, quick fix - there is rigour and you will find yourself being challenged as you peel away the layers, examine, and then re-shape time management on your home front. This is a contemporary process to help you track, rate and cost your time, and then set up a series of simple and sustainable solutions to manage your time smarter.

So, shift your gaze from the view out your window and focus - here is what you are in for and this is how you will get back 30 hours a month of quality time. Yes!

The 5 Steps to Being SMART

So, let's talk SMART:

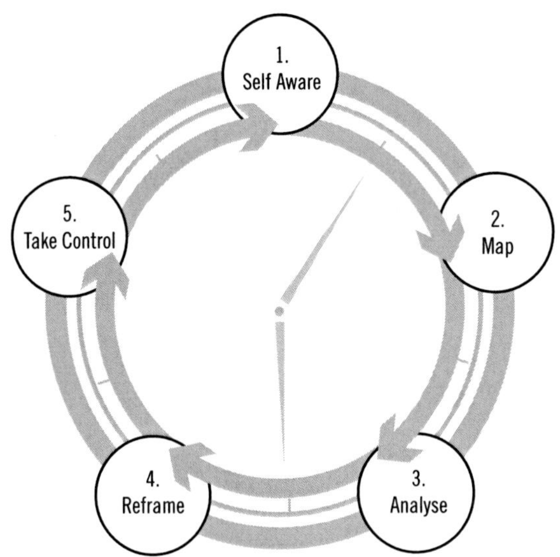

S = SELF AWARE

The first step to getting back genuine quality time, SELF AWARE, will help you identify and understand:

- your key time management problems
- your Values and Priorities.

M = MAP

You will MAP out a Standard Day and a Dream Day in detail - to see where you currently spend your time and where you would like to spend your time.

A = ANALYSE

You will ANALYSE your time across four categories - Musts, Wants, Delegates, and Rejects, and identify what your current time management habits are costing you.

R = REFRAME

This where the work you have done in the first 3 steps comes together. REFRAME has you re-assess your Delegates and Rejects and reframe your Musts and Wants.

T = TAKE CONTROL

TAKE CONTROL establishes your Action Plan to ensure you implement and then sustain your new time management behaviours.

Supported with tools and advice, this is where the rubber hits the road!

> The *5 Steps to Being SMART* underpins how you will get back significant amounts of lost time each month. The sooner you commence the *5 Steps to Being SMART*, the sooner you will have the extra quality time and the balance, freedom, success, family time, or *Me Time* you want.

So, are you ready to get back 30 hours a month?

◇◇

Alice's Me Time Diary

I cannot believe I forgot to take a plate of cupcakes for the school stall. And now it's too late to dash to the supermarket to buy a packet of cakes because everyone saw me turn up empty-handed and they will know I CHEATED (and then maybe they will realise that I cheated last time too ...). Besides I have to get to my 9.30am meeting.

Who comes up with these ridiculous ideas anyway? Why do we need to have a school stall to raise money for 'Iguanas in danger'? I don't care about iguanas. Who knew they were in danger? Why the extra pressure? Honestly it would be easier if I just wrote the school a cheque for $200:

'Here you are, you evil setter-upper of failure for mums masquerading as a bastion of education - a cheque for 200 cakes right there! I didn't cook any (I forgot, again), but I am very happy to buy the lot! Hurrah!'

Why can't I remember these things? I know why, because I have 10 bazillion things chasing each other around my head.

I don't know what's worse - the look of disappointment on Olive's face, the looks of pity on the other mums' faces, or the teacher's pursed lips. When Sarah offered to share her 'home made' muffins with Olive could the ground not have opened up and swallowed me whole?

Damn, damn, damn.

Can't you just teach my child to read, write and count? Is testing the agility and ability of the mother and then holding her up to the scrutiny of the school community now on the curriculum too?

Bad mum. Bad mum. Bad mum.

Stress and guilt. Love it. I just wish I had more time. More head space.

Imagine if I found those 30 hours a month. Ohhh ... But, can I park my stress and guilt long enough to do this? I know the way I think - even if I get back hours of time, I will probably just feel tormented over how I should actually spend that time. I will probably ... Damn it Alice! Just get over it. Time is money and it's time to put my money where my mouth is.

Okay.

◇◇

Your Commitment

I can tell you how to get back 30 hours a month but I can't make you do it. That's up to you. You are in the driver's seat for this journey. And just like any road trip there will be times when you simply zoom along and enjoy the view and then there will be times when you wonder why the hell you didn't just fly instead.

As you journey through *Me Time* you may be tempted to give it all up. When that happens, come back and read this section. If you want 30 hours plus back a month, you need to commit to staying the course.

Managing your time smarter is going to present some challenges - you know it - for example:

- Stopping bad time management habits and establishing new better time management habits won't happen overnight - the process in *Me Time* will take 30 days to establish.
- Maintaining the 30 hours you save by implementing the *5 Steps to Being SMART* is an ongoing journey. Beyond the 30 days you need to implement your changes, continue to revisit the process, and hone your new time management skills to save even more time. You will make the most of your time every month by regularly checking back and testing that you are using your time in the best possible way.
- Every now and then your priorities will change. When this occurs you need to have the flexibility to recalibrate.
- You might start to doubt your choices or start with negative self-talk or let the judgement of others wear you down.

I want you to commit right now to staying the course.

Exercise - Your Commitment

The *Me Time* Workbook includes a Commitment Certificate, also set out below. Print it out, fill it in and paste it on the wall next to your computer in your office at work or at home.

Purpose

It's time to commit. This is a journey. You will hit some pot holes. You will need some rest stops. And you will wonder from time to time why you are travelling this road. By committing, in writing, you will make this road trip real for yourself.

My Commitment Certificate

I .... commit to properly implementing the *5 Steps to Being SMART,* or at least doing a pretty good job because I really do want 30 hours back a month to do what I love and even though I might have times when I am feeling really cynical or jaded or sick of yelling at my partner or my kids to pick up their crap or my mother-in-law tells me she has never paid someone to clean her home or I start to think I am a bit of a failure for not doing everything myself or .... (insert 100 other excuses), I promise myself that I will stay the course and put my money where my mouth is because I WANT 30 HOURS BACK A MONTH AND DAMN IT I AM GOING TO GET THEM!

Signed .... Date ....

Judgement time

— *What other women say* —

Natasha Stott Despoja AM, Former Leader of the Australian Democrats, Australia's Ambassador for Women and Girls and founding Chairperson of the Foundation to Prevent Violence Against Women and their Children

… the best thing we can do as women is support each other, not judge each other's choices.

Carolyn Creswell, Founder Carman's

With parenting, a lot of people do judge you. At school I might not be in the kiosk or the uniform shop, but I will be working with the Principal on a new project for the school. I might not be as 'visible' to some parents. But you just have to say 'This is the right journey for me and my family, and we are happy'.

Janine Allis, Founder and Managing Director Boost Juice (Retail Zoo)

Maybe I have been judged, I haven't really noticed. You can't change what other people think of you. But you do have a choice – you can dwell on it or you can choose not to care.

The judgement that comes our way for our life choices is endless. If you work as well as being a mum, you judge yourself and others judge you. If you stay at home with your kids, you judge yourself and others judge you. If you work part time, you judge yourself and others judge you. If you work full time, you judge yourself and others judge you. You are judged as being amazing for doing it all or as being a machine for the same reason. You are damned if you do and damned if you don't, or just plain damned.

Let's address this nonsense once and for all.

For those of you who judge yourself, that destructive little voice in your head might already have started up its chatter. Yes? I will come to self-talk in a minute.

For others, it might be the looks or comments you get from other women, including those closest to you (the ones who should be most supportive of you) that will start to wear you down. You may even be criticised for reading *Me Time*. So, when criticism comes your way be armed with some lovely sassy responses that will leave you feeling empowered as opposed to crushed. Here are some examples to practise:

'Mum! FFS! You can criticise me for getting a housekeeper OR you can choose to celebrate how proud you are that your daughter is pulling in big dollars as a successful career woman and building quality time into her family life as well. Do you honestly expect me to do it all, by myself? Just because you manage your life in a particular way, it doesn't mean that everyone has to follow your course. I'd actually like you to be on my side in this one Mum. Stop judging me.'

~

'You know what, Helen? I've worked my guts out climbing the corporate ladder and I am really good at what I do. I am immensely proud of where I am today. I've had to make hard choices and there have been trade-offs, but I am making more time for my family now through some intelligent time management. But, you know what? Cutting down tall poppies doesn't leave you standing tall! No.

And, as my good friend for so many years, I actually look to you to cheer me on. To be proud of what I have done. I want you to be on my side in this one. Please.'

~

'Come on ladies, lighten up! Stop judging your daughters, your friends, your sisters, your acquaintances and your colleagues. If you can't stop, then at least spend a little time in the room of mirrors before you are tempted to criticise. Ask yourself: Am I really so perfect and amazing that I am in a position to make another woman feel guilty about her life choices?'

There will always be naysayers to every decision you make. Too bad - it's your life.

Destructive self-talk is another beast all together. You know you do it. As you are reading this, a nagging little voice in your head might be starting to get your attention. It might be telling you that you actually do need to *do it all*. And hand in hand with the destructive self-chatter comes an overwhelming sense of guilt. Then along comes the stress. Yay - the trifecta of self-doubt!

Me Time is not a book about how to manage your guilt or your stress. There are plenty of books out there dealing with those big hairy problems. This isn't one of them. I will, however, touch on guilt and stress in a tough love kind of way. That's because I am a tough love, time-saving crusader, and quite frankly your guilt is getting in your way.

There are lots of types of guilt and associated stress some of you might be feeling right about now.

81% of the women I ask tell me they are *stressed* while 65% of the same women tell me they regularly feel *guilty*.

— What other women say —

Angela Counsel, Business & Lifestyle Coach and Author

I used to feel guilty because I wasn't feeling guilty enough about working!

Me Time is going to help you reframe your day, freeing you up to reallocate your time and remove some of your stress and guilt. You will adopt new behaviours and take new actions to change your overall environment for the better. If your stress and guilt become overwhelming, remind yourself of these two simple facts:

- If you action the *5 Steps to Being SMART* from start to finish you will get back at least 30 hours a month.
- If you allow yourself to be overcome by stress and guilt over the changes you are making to the way you manage your time, you will NOT get back the time. You will lose focus, or you won't complete the *5 Steps to Being SMART* properly, or you will give up.

Hence this is an intervention. Every time you hear that seductive little voice whispering words of guilt in your ear, or tugging longingly at your heart strings, or crushing your spirit, or raising your levels of stress, or every time you catch a sideways look in your direction, pursed lips of disapproval or open criticism about the choices you are making to help manage your time, come back and read this section again. And then, again.

You can't stop other people judging you, but you can stop judging yourself.

Listen to this voice instead:

I am an incredible woman – dynamic, successful and clever. And yet, I have been setting the bar so high that I have set myself up to fail. I will stop listening to the criticism. I will dial the chatter in my brain to a more positive channel. If I want a cleaner, I will get a cleaner. If I want an ironer, I will get an ironer. If I need to supply muffins for school then I will buy them from the supermarket. If I want to skydive in the nude, I will! I am going to give myself a break. I am doing a great job. And if I can't stop feeling guilty and stressed, then I am going to try my hardest to put it to one side just for now or this process won't work. Besides, I've signed the Commitment Certificate so now I'm locked in.

OK?

— *What other women say* —

Tanya McVicar, Head of Operational Risk & Compliance, Personal Banking at National Australia Bank

As I was reframing my time with the 5 Steps to Being SMART, it was critical for me to build in time with my daughters. Between them, there are probably three dozen school events I could attend each year. However, I work full time in a demanding job. Attending 36 school events was never going to happen. This used to stress me out and I felt enormous guilt. Other mums turned up all the time, didn't they?

But after working through the 5 Steps to Being SMART, I had a different perspective. I selected the big ticket items for me and my girls – things like the Easter Bonnet Parade, the Inter-School Sports Day, and any school assembly where the girls might receive a school award or acknowledgement. The things that I don't want to miss out on. By choosing the cream of the events to attend, I now feel involved and that I'm not missing out. It also helps me manage work expectations. In most cases, I am only away from work for an hour and a half. My kids love it and so do I.

Carolyn Creswell, Founder Carman's

I don't feel guilty about my choices. With my kids, I choose what is most important to them. Recently I didn't get to a school assembly where my son was receiving a certificate, but I explained to him that my husband would be there, that he would take photos and we would celebrate together that night. The important thing for him was that celebration and connection in the evening. It's not the number of hours you spend, it's the quality of time and giving your child 100% focus at that time.

Janine Allis, Founder and Managing Director Boost Juice (Retail Zoo)

I'm the mother other women hang out with to make themselves feel good about their parenting! But I threw guilt away. I never feel guilty about not doing all the school stuff. Who would I be pleasing by being there? The other mums – and do I really care about pleasing them? I only do something if it actually involves me being together with one of my kids, like working side by side at the sausage sizzle. It gets down to what is most important to my kids. If they really want me there, then I will be there.

The Secret 6th Step – the Power of Collaboration

Your first instinct might be to put up the shutters and deal with transforming your time all on your own. However, don't underestimate the power of collaboration.

If you decide you need some additional help or if you think you will get your best results by working with others, then tap into your personal network and collaborate on this stuff.

You have a lot of people around you that know how you tick, with a point of view on your strengths and weaknesses, and the changes you might need to make to manage your time smarter. So grab a group of friends, read *Me Time* together and tap into their rich vein of advice.

Nice Work. Now You Know:

- The 7 most common time management mistakes busy, clever women make
- How to say *No*
- The basics of the *5 Steps to Being SMART*
- That getting time back will take your commitment
- That you might judge yourself, or others might judge you (so, what's new?)
- That you might like to collaborate on this journey.

It's time to become SELF AWARE.

PART 2

THE *5 STEPS TO BEING SMART*

STEP 1: SELF AWARE

The first step to getting back genuine quality time requires a moment or two of self-reflection. Step 1, Self Aware, is designed to gently introduce you to the *5 Steps to Being SMART* by helping you identify and understand:

- your key time management problems
- your Values and Priorities.

◇◇

Alice's Me Time Diary

Ho Hum. Am I Self Aware? How do I feel? Is this really necessary? Where do I start ... ? Can I lie down for this?

It's 10pm. I need a wine. God I'm tired. Oh dear, now John wants to talk about his day. Maybe if I just sit here and quietly sip my wine and nod every now and then and make noises like 'oh, yes, aha, yep, no', he will think I'm listening.

I have to remember to set my alarm for 6am so I can make the school lunches before I head out to my breakfast meeting. I'm going to wear my white dress, I can wear it with my black shoes, that always looks hot to trot. Put phone on charger. Oh damn it, Henry has assembly tomorrow.

I promised him I would go. Shit it. I'll call Mum in the morning to see if she can go and watch.

I can't believe that email, I need to get on to that first thing. Roast chicken for dinner tomorrow. I can pick up the chook after my lunch meeting. Henry has footy training and Olive has basketball; I might be able to share drop-off and pick-up with Suzi. Maybe I can watch football training to make up for missing assembly?

'Yes Honey I agree'.

Need cat food and milk. Cereal. Dry cleaning. House looks like a bomb has gone off. If I leave the dishes until tomorrow, hopefully someone else will do them. Yeah right. Interstate next week for 2 days; check with Mum to do those days for me. Or maybe John can do them? I need to catch up with the team tomorrow and set up that new internet protocol. Damn, I forgot to call Henry's teacher back; I hope it's nothing bad.

'Honey I just remembered Henry's teacher called, can you call her tomorrow? Plus don't forget you are on school drop-off tomorrow. Yes I did tell you. I told you on Tuesday. Yes I did. I told you I have a breakfast meeting. Yes I did!'

'For God's sake John, I can't do it all!'

◇◇

Have I lost my mind?

You are very busy. You are being pulled in many different directions by many different people. You have competing priorities and responsibilities. You are trying your best to get everything done and (mostly) you do it all (fairly) well.

It's hard.

When it comes to managing time, and keeping all those balls in the air, most successful women will have some key pain points that challenge them again and again. The three most common are:

1. They don't have enough time to manage all of their competing priorities. And time for themselves? Forget it.
2. They feel guilty about the work/life choices they make – that they are spending too much time on their career or their business at the expense of their family.
3. They worry that they can't be successful at work and at home.

There are lots of other pain points, but these are the ones that come up most frequently.

Your pain points will change depending on what stage you are at in your career or business, the age of your children, whether you are in a relationship, if you are a single mum (or virtually so) and so on.

— *What other women say* —

Natasha Stott Despoja AM, Former Leader of the Australian Democrats, Australia's Ambassador for Women and Girls and founding Chairperson of the Foundation to Prevent Violence Against Women and their Children

Like many people, my biggest problem is time: there's never enough.

There are different challenges depending on the work I am doing: when I am travelling (I spend up to a quarter of each month overseas now as Ambassador for Women and Girls), the challenge is to organise things as far in advance as possible (school casual days/baby-sitting/birthday gifts/

Spanish Day costumes/sports pick-ups etc) so that things run relatively smoothly. My husband, Ian, and I work out diaries three months in advance.

When I am in Australia, I often work from my home office in Adelaide, so the challenge is delineating between work and family time. Trying to write speeches, draft emails, have meetings or take conference calls while juggling kids is near impossible.

Work/life balance - like happiness - is somewhat elusive but we do the best we can.

Exercise - Sanity Check

Purpose

There are 4 exercises below. Their purpose is to give you the space for a little self-reflection. As a busy woman, self-reflection is not something you do often. Funnily enough, it's partly because you don't have the time, but it is also because a healthy session of self-reflection can be pretty confronting. But, it's time to walk into the room of mirrors and take a good hard look to see how you actually feel about this life you are living.

Exercise 1 - My key Time Management Challenges

The three things I find most challenging when it comes to managing my time:

1. ______________________________

2. ______________________________

3. ______________________________

You can use the list below as a guide, or add your own unique challenges.

I don't have enough time to manage all of my competing priorities.

I feel guilty that I am spending too much time on my career or my business at the expense of my family and other priorities.

I can't be successful at work and at home.

I can't give 100% effort to all of the things I do.

I don't stop and settle my mind.

I find my work challenging and stimulating and it's hard for me to switch off.

I find it hard to use my time productively.

I waste my time on silly things.

I always put myself last: work; family; home; me – the pyramid is inverted!

I procrastinate when it comes to decision making.
I struggle to manage other people's expectations.
I don't schedule time for myself.
I don't have a support network.
I don't spend enough time with my kids.
I don't spend enough time with my partner.
I don't get enough sleep.
I feel like I am constantly letting people down.
I take on too much, I just can't say No.
I know it's just quicker to do it myself.

These are some of the time management problems *Me Time* will help you resolve.

— *What other women say* —

Nicola Moras, Kickass Marketing Mentor

My biggest pain point? I am addicted to my business, I love it but I find it very challenging to stop and put it aside. I also find it challenging to use the limited time I have as productively as possible.

Amy Poynton, Business Advisor, Board Member (retired partner Ernst & Young)

Sometimes I just need to stop reacting. Press the pause button and think 'what am I doing?' Every now and then I feel overwhelmed. I need to take a one minute pause, breathe, clear my mind, and then move on.

Alice's Me Time Diary

The three things I find most challenging when it comes to managing my time:

Being completely honest here, I would say that I have way more than 3 top challenges when it comes to managing my time. In fact, I would say I have a top 25 challenges. Pretty much every one of those mentioned above, plus a few more. Try throwing in frustration, anger, fatigue, temper tantrums (mine).

Righto, here are the 3 which I guess are my biggest pain points:

1. *I don't have enough time. Ever.*
2. *I am constantly guilty about the amount of time I spend at work at the expense of my kids.*
3. *I'm too tired to change how I manage my time.*

That's a good start. Now, let's dig a little deeper.

Exercise 2 - How Do I Feel Right Now?

Answer the questions in Column 1 with a *Yes* or *No*. Work quickly down that column and trust your first instinct. Then reflect on your answers and write down your thoughts in Column 2.

	Column 1	Column 2
	Yes/No	Why/Why Not?
Are you stress free?		
Are you guilt free?		
Are you happy?		

	Column 1	Column 2
	Yes/No	Why/Why Not?
Do you feel calm?		
Do you have balance across all aspects of your life?		
Are you energised?		
Are you healthy?		
Are you fit?		
Do you have enough time?		
Do you feel in control of your life?		
Are you focussed?		
Do you feel content?		
Are your relationships healthy?		
Is your business/career going well?		
Do you spend time on yourself?		
Are you able to live in the moment?		
	Total Yes: /16	

Unless you have a Yes for most of the above questions then it's time to make some changes. You are a clever woman but you are not being smart about the way you manage your life. If your response rate is leaning towards the No's, these are the feelings you want to shift to Yes by the end of *Me Time*.

Alice's Me Time Diary

	Column 1	Column 2
	Yes/No	Why/Why Not?
Are you stress free?	*No*	*Of course not. I am stressed out. I have too much on my plate and no down time. Sometimes I wake up in the middle of the night and lie in a cold sweat of stress-induced insomnia. I am not stressFREE, I am stressFULL*
Are you guilt free?	*No*	*Aren't all working mums guilt-ridden? I don't do enough with my kids. I don't do enough with my husband. I never see my friends. I hardly see my parents. I feel guilty leaving work before the 'non mums'. If there is something to be guilty about I will find it. I was born guilty.*
Are you happy?	*Yes*	*I am happy when I am at work and it is going well. I am happy when I have quality time with my family. But I feel a level of dissatisfaction with the way I am living my life. On the whole, 'mostly happy' sums me up.*
Do you feel calm?	*No*	*I yell. A lot. I feel angry. John drives me crazy when he doesn't pick up the slack. Then I feel guilty for resenting him. And I don't communicate this and it builds up and then I blow.*
Do you have balance across all aspects of your life?	*No*	*What is work/life balance? I wish someone could give me a definition that I understand. It sounds so unrealistic.*
Are you energised?	*No*	*I am tired all the time. I wake up tired.*
Are you healthy?	*No*	*I am fit, but I wouldn't say I am healthy. I drink too much alcohol - sometimes I just watch that clock tick towards 6pm so that I can open a bottle of wine. I drink too much coffee. Mentally I am just so tired. I am stressed. Things worry me. I have bad days. No, I don't think I am healthy. I'd like to be healthier.*
Are you fit?	*Yes*	*Jogging is the one thing I do for me. Yes, I am fit. In fact, if it wasn't for being fit I don't think I could get through my day!*
Do you have enough time?	*No*	*Because I am a bloody busy woman juggling a full-time career, with 2 kids, a house to run, a husband, 2 pets, a holiday to plan, dishes to do, washing to wash, dinners to cook, lunches to make, and 1000 other responsibilities. Jeez.*

	Column 1	Column 2
	Yes/No	Why/Why Not?
Do you feel in control of your life?	*No*	*I don't think I am in total control of my life. The thing is, I am great at responding to things which are thrown my way but to be honest that just means I am dancing to other people's agendas. But, I do have choices available to me. If I was truly unhappy or felt like control had slipped completely over to the dark side, I guess I would make other choices. On the whole, not in as much control as I'd like to be.*
Are you focussed?	*No*	*When I am in the zone at work I am definitely focussed. The rest of the time I am anything but focussed. I would describe myself as manic.*
Do you feel content?	*Yes*	*I have a great job, I have awesome kids, I love John, my family are healthy. I am just so tired. And I would like more time. But I am content - life could obviously be a lot worse.*
Are your relationships healthy?	*Yes*	*I know I need to learn to switch off and focus when I am with the kids. I need more 1:1 time with John. When was the last time we had a proper conversation that didn't involve coordinating our schedules? But generally speaking things are OK. My work relationships are healthy. I neglect my friends. And my parents! OMG, they almost never figure in my life these days I am so busy.*
Is your business/ career going well?	*Yes*	*All good. I love my job. Flying. Just bloody guilty because I feel like I am anything but successful at home. Failure is probably too strong a word. Isn't it?*
Do you spend time on yourself?	*No*	*I squeeze in 3x 30 minute jogs a week. That's it.*
Are you able to live in the moment?	*No*	*Sorry - what did you say? Ha! Good one Alice.*
	Total Yes: 5/16	

Oh dear. 5 out of 16 isn't too good. Guess I'm not being smart about the way I live. Ho Hum.

Exercise 3 - What One Thing Would I Change?

Review your answers to the above questions, have a think about your comments and then answer these questions:

How do your comments above make you feel?

____

____

____

If you could fix one of the above which would you choose, and why?

____

____

____

Alice's Me Time Diary

How do your comments make you feel?

Not great. I really need to make some changes. It's actually pretty bloody depressing, self-reflecting. But, in a weird way it's funny too. Funny that I have just been zooming along so fast that I haven't taken the time to sit down and think about my life. About whether I am happy, content, calm, enjoying myself. I haven't asked myself these questions before. Ever. And now that I have, I feel like I have opened Pandora's Box.

~

If you could fix one of the above which would you choose, and why?

I choose MORE TIME! Thinking this through and reflecting on my answers, not having enough time really seems to be the root of all of my other pain points.

If I had more time, I could spend some of it on my kids which would reduce how guilty I feel. And if I had more time then I could reorganise my life, give myself more 'me' time and maybe get back some energy. And if I had more time I could lose that sensation of always rushing from one thing to the next, chasing my goddamned tail to get it all done. And if I had more time I could sit in the sun for an hour on the weekend drinking a gin & tonic while reading that crime novel that has been sitting on my bedside table for 2 years. And . . . yes, More Time would be nice.

— What other women say —

Christie Nicholas, Director, Kids Business Communications

What would I change? I would love more time. I talk with a lot of professional women who are also mums. Everyone I talk to agrees that more time would be good!

Well, now you know

This is not all doom and gloom. I don't want you to look at the above exercises and your responses, admit defeat and curl up into a small ball under your chair. It's OK to admit you are not living the dream. The whole idea of doing these exercises in Step 1 Self Aware is so you know where you are at, right now. Plus, once you get back 30 hours a month you can look back to see how far you have come.

This is good. Breathe.

You can see that change is needed. Give yourself permission to make that change. Understand and agree that you do not need to be Superwoman. Understand and agree that if you don't at least tweak your time management habits you will not be the best person that you can be, and getting to the next level of success in your career or business will be much harder to achieve and sustain. You will continue to be under-productive. You will continue to be unhappy, or stressed, or guilty, or angry or whatever the feelings are that you have identified above.

What I really, really want

As a highly successful woman you are driven, you work hard, and you love the buzz of each win you have at work. The downside of this is that it can be hard to flick the switch to *Off* to spend some of your time on things which aren't work related. For good or bad, work is your drug of choice.

However, as you are about to get back hours of genuine quality time to live the life you want *(Hell yeah Baby!)*, wouldn't it be nice to spend some of your reclaimed hours on pursuits other than your work?

So let's make this real. Make a Wants List of what you are going to do with your 30 hours.

Some of you will have a ready-made mental Wants List a foot long. But if not, if it has been simply too long since you put yourself first, then the following broad categories might assist:

1. Me time - just me, me, me and no-one else
2. Family and friends
3. Personal growth or further education
4. Physical, emotional, mental or spiritual health
5. Growing your career or business.

Exercise 4 - What Will I Do With 30 Extra Hours a Month?

This is to remind yourself that you are now on a very simple, but bloody exciting, mission to get back 30 hours a month.

Think about your closest friends who are also mums, but who don't seem to be as time poor as you. Write a list of all the things they do which are not work-related. Think about their hobbies, interests, pursuits, classes, sports, what they do with their friends, what they do with their kids, what they do with their partners, and what they do as a family. Thinking about this list, which items resonate with you - ask yourself '*Is this something I would enjoy doing if I had the time?*' If *yes*, put it on your own Wants List.

> ***Understand and agree that if you don't find and then allocate time to yourself you may well go mad.***

Other women who have followed the *5 Steps to Being SMART* identify some great items for their Wants Lists, which might also give you food for thought, including:

Girl time	Play board games	Meditate
Build a new house	Read	Return to study
More exercise	Help my kids with homework	Socialise more
Time with my kids	Attend more school events	Take up a hobby
Plan an overseas trip	Shopping	Find a partner
Self-development	Just sit	Facials
More time with my family	Read the paper	Regular massages
Holidays	Gardening	Get my nails done
Yoga	Travel	Learn Italian
Learn to cook	Learn to drive	Sing
Get fit	Rock climb	Sleep
Weekly date night	Have sex with my husband	Read my book
Go for a walk	Surf	Play the piano
Learn to play the flute	Learn the viola	Practise my French
Sit in the sun	Go to the movies	Get my hair done
Cuddle on the couch	Adventures with my family	Take an art class
Volunteer work	Play golf	Learn to skate

— *What other women say* —

Nicola Moras, Kickass Marketing Mentor

You need to do something outside of work and family and your business. Just for you. Carve it out of your diary and do it. For me, it's Roller Derby. Create time for yourself or you will go insane. It's so important to give back to yourself.

Holly Kramer, CEO Best & Less

I steal time where I can, and its pure escapism – a pedicure with a magazine, watching a movie or reading a book.

Janine Allis, Founder and Managing Director Boost Juice (Retail Zoo)

Between the age of 30 and 40, I was growing my business. Consequently I had no friends and little Me Time. I had my business, my husband and my kids. It had to be that way. Now, well Me Time for me is on a yoga mat, hanging out with friends (I have friends now!), sitting on a beach, surfing, playing with horses.

Christie Nicholas, Director, Kids Business Communications

I used to spend more time on myself but this has gone out the window to accommodate growing work, family and life demands. I would like to refocus on this as a way to feel more balanced with life. My goal is to dedicate more time to a personal, creative outlet.

My Wants List: What I will do with my 30 hours a month?

◇◇

Alice's Me Time Diary

My Wants List: What I will do with my 30 hours a month?

~ *Take up boxing*

~ *Learn meditation*

~ *Do a barista course*

~ *Teach the kids to cook without yelling*

~ *Hit the shops with a vengeance and update my wardrobe*

~ *Jog more regularly*

~ *Get a lover (Just kidding John - I thought you might be snooping . . .)*

~ *Plan a family holiday - an adventure involving crocodiles*

Ummm ...

◇◇

Take a copy of your Wants List and put it on your fridge, next to your computer, behind the toilet door - or anywhere you spend a bit of time thinking. We will come back to this in Step 4 Reframe.

What floats your boat?

You have started your Wants List, which will also help you in identifying your Values.

Your Values are what you stand for - the principles, beliefs and moral compass which guide your decisions, including how you choose to spend your time. They help you identify what is most important to you so you can establish your priorities, focus your time and effort, and stop chasing the distractions.

You don't have the time to do everything, so it makes sense to focus on what is important. By articulating your Values, you will have a pretty good idea of the people, the work, and the lifestyle outcomes you most want to spend your time on.

Put it another way - if you aren't clear on your Values, how on earth do you expect to identify the distractions which you can discard as a drain on your time?

So, what are your Values?

This answer will be different for every single woman who reads *Me Time*. It's your life, your family and your career or business, so don't look at Superwoman and wonder what floats her boat.

— *What other women say* —

Janine Allis, Founder and Managing Director Boost Juice (Retail Zoo)

I think that a happy working woman is a better mother, wife and person. But it's all about choice. Some of my best friends are stay at home mums and they love it. Do what makes you happy.

Defining your Values

The Values by which you live are ingrained. They have been part of you since you were little - for example, as a child:

- did you ever intervene in a schoolyard push-and-shove fest because you thought the odds weren't even? (your Values are likely to include: Fairness and Courage);
- did you keep putting your hand up to run the cross-country even though you knew you would never win? (your Values are likely to include: Resilience, Determination and Perseverance).

Have you thought about what is most important to you now as a woman? If your automatic response is family time and yet you work around the clock, travel for work, and rarely see your family, then you are either kidding yourself (your Values are more closely associated with success at work), or you are living with terrible guilt because your work/life choices are not aligned to your Values.

So where do you stand?

— *What other women say* —

Angela Counsel, Business & Lifestyle Coach and Author

When my kids were little I couldn't count the number of hours I was working a week. I lived and breathed my work. I had decided to focus on growing my business, but in fact my focus was not there, my focus was on my kids. So I constantly felt guilty because I wasn't living my values. I wasn't being honest with myself.

You need to be very clear about what you really want.

Janine Allis, Founder and Managing Director Boost Juice (Retail Zoo)

Fear used to be a huge component of what drove me. I had everything on the line. It was the fear of failure. The fear I would be caught out as not knowing what I was doing. It was almost debilitating. I would forward project and plan for every possible outcome. The up side was that we never ran out of money, and I could deal with most challenges that came my way because I had planned for them!

Exercise - Your Values

Purpose

There are 4 exercises below. Their purpose is to help you identify and clearly articulate your Values. Be honest. Your answers are unique to you and stuff it what anyone else thinks - this isn't a competition over who is the best mum or best career women or best entrepreneur or who has the best values.

To help you complete this exercise you might like to use the Values Table below which includes lots of different, typical values.

Values Examples:

Adventurous	Efficient	Independent	Self-controlled
Ambitious	Empathetic	[Of] integrity	Selfless
Assertive	Enthusiastic	Intelligent	Self-reliant
Balanced	Ethical	Just	Sensitive
Brave	Expert	Kind	Spiritual
Calm	Fair	Knowledgeable	Spontaneous
Caring	Faithful	Loved	Strategic
Committed	Family-oriented	Loving	Strong
Community-minded	Financially-secure	Loyal	Successful
		Original	Supportive
Compassionate	Fit	Patient	Talented
Competitive	Focussed	Positive	Team-oriented
Consistent	Frugal	Powerful	Thoughtful
Contented	Fun	Practical	Trustworthy
Cooperative	Generous	Private	Understanding
Courageous	Giving	Professional	Unique
Creative	Good	Prudent	Valiant
Curious	Happy	Reliable	Visionary
Dependable	Hard-working	Resilient	Virtuous
Determined	Healthy	Resourceful	Well-regarded
Diligent	Helpful	Respected	Wise
Discreet	Honest	Responsible	

Exercise 1 - What's Important to Me?

To help identify your Values - what is most important to you - complete the following sentences.

Next, read each of your statements and assign an adjective(s) which best describes what it says about you. For example, if you wrote, 'I like watching my family having fun' you could say that this means you are 'family-oriented'. If you wrote 'good food and nutrition' you could say that this means you are 'health-conscious':

Sentence	Your response	Value
I am at my happiest when …		
I get a deep feeling of satisfaction when …		
I would spend a spare free hour on …		
If I won $1000, I would spend it on …		
I feel most energised when I am …		
In my favourite room I surround myself with …		
When I daydream, I dream about …		
If I were to receive a compliment, I'd want it to be …		
When I initiate a conversation, I love to talk about …		
My best days ever were …		
The things I won't compromise on are …		

Alice's Me Time Diary

Sentence	Your response	Value
I am at my happiest when …	*I'm jogging* *I win @ work* *Getting a bonus or pay-rise* *My kids are happy & don't fight* *Spending time with John*	*Fit, Healthy, Independent* *Successful, Integrity, Ethical* *Financially secure, Successful* *Family-oriented* *Family-oriented, Loved*
I get a deep feeling of satisfaction when …	*I'm productive @ work* *I contribute to the Vision of my firm* *I deliver on promises* *My kids are happy* *John has a win he is proud of*	*Successful, Professional, Financially secure* *Team oriented, Integrity, Ethical* *Integrity, Honest, Ethical* *Loving, Loved, Caring* *Loving, Caring, Competitive*
I would spend a spare free hour on …	*A jog* *Cleaning the house* *Working* *Supermarket*	*Fit, Healthy, Independent* *Hard-working, Dependable,* *Crazy, Ambitious, Hard-working* *Hungry (ha!)*
If I won $1000, I would spend it on …	*The house* *A family adventure* *Clothes & shoes*	*Successful, Family-oriented, Financially secure* *Family-oriented, Adventurous, Financially secure* *Spontaneous, Fun*
I feel most energised when I am …	*Exercising* *Winning @ work* *Enjoying my family* *Successful both @ work & home*	*Fit, Healthy, Independent* *Ambitious, Expert, Well-regarded, Financially secure* *Loving, Loved, Caring, Family-oriented* *Successful, Contented*
In my favourite room I surround myself with …	*Awards from work* *Books I love, Art* *Family photos* *The wonderful crap from the Mother's Day stall*	*Well-regarded, Expert, Successful* *Caring, Loving, Contented* *Hard-working, Successful, Financially secure* *Loving, Loved, Caring, Family-oriented* *Loving, Loved, Caring, Family-oriented*

Sentence	Your response	Value
When I daydream, I dream about …	*Winning a new client* *Our next holiday* *A weekend away with John* *Sleeping in* *My house being automated to clean and cook all by itself*	*Ambitious, Successful, Competitive, Financially secure* *Adventurous, Family-oriented* *Loved, Loving* *Healthy, Indulgent!* *Wishful, Deluded*
If I were to receive a compliment, I'd want it to be …	*'You are a great mum'* *'You are a wonderful role model for young women'* *'You look hot today' (yes, I do, don't I)*	*Well-regarded, Respected,* *Well-regarded, Respected,* *Expert, Successful, Professional* *Deluded*
When I initiate a conversation, I love to talk about …	*New clients, work* *Good restaurants* *My kids* *Who is sleeping around (snort!)*	*Ambitious, Successful, Competitive* *Food-loving, Healthy* *Family-oriented, and to be honest – competitive! Oh dear!* *Naughty*
My best days ever were …	*My wedding* *Kids' births* *Running half marathon* *Buying our house*	*Loving, Loved* *Loving, Loved, Caring, Family-oriented* *Fit, Successful* *Successful, Financially secure*
The things I won't compromise on are …	*Good food & nutrition* *Success @ work* *Being challenged @ work* *Quality time with kids* *Family birthdays* *Work deadlines* *Family's health*	*Fit, Healthy, Food-loving* *Ambitious, Expert, Successful* *Competitive, Expert* *Family-oriented, Loving, Caring* *As above* *Respected, Well-regarded, Dependable, Expert* *Family-oriented, Loving, Caring*

Your answers above will give you a strong sense of what is most important to you. By understanding this, you can avoid wasting your time on the things which simply have little or no value to you.

Exercise 2 - The Common Threads

There will be some common threads running through your answers. Review your answers and think about what they have in common. Label these common threads with a word which encapsulates them as a Value:

My Values:

◇◇

Alice's Me Time Diary

My Values:

Adventurous	*Competitive*	*Integrity*
Successful	*Empathetic*	*Family-oriented*
Professional	*Independent*	
Ambitious	*Ethical*	*Expert*
Loved	*Hard-working*	*Fit*
Caring	*Fun*	*Healthy*
Dependable	*Well-regarded*	*Loving*
Financially secure	*Respected*	
Talented		
Honest		

◇◇

Exercise 3 - My Top Values

You will have many Values, most of which will remain consistent throughout your life and some of which will change depending on your stage of life. Knowing which of your Values are the most important to you, helps ensure you make time-based decisions which are consistent with your Values.

Based on the Values you have identified in Exercise 2 above, distil your list down to your 6-8 Top Values. This will be challenging. You may have identified 20 Values which resonate strongly with you. If so, undertake

Exercise 3 in two parts - boil it down to 12-15 Values now, and then revisit your list in a few days' time, after you have mulled it over, and have another cull to get your list down to under 10.

My Top Values:

◇◇

Alice's Me Time Diary

Damn it, I have 24. How am I supposed to get it down to 10 or less? Who knew I was so Values oriented?

But really, who am I kidding? I'm not fun. Do I value fun? I'd like to be fun, but I don't have the time. OK. Lose Fun. Loving and Loved - both are important to me, but I guess Loving is more important. Lose Loved. In terms of work I have Ambitious; Professional; Successful; Hard-working; Expert; Dependable; Respected; Talented; Well-regarded. I can see a common thread here -ha! Having success is more important to me than having ambition - I am ambitious but I think the desire for success drives me harder than pure ambition. Lose Ambitious, same for Talented.

Dependable makes me sound like I'm a Labrador. Lose Hard-working, that's just a given.

OK, I'm down to 18. Bloody hell. This is hard. Clearly 'Decisive' is not one of my Values.

Loving is stronger than Caring for me. Lose Caring. Is it cheating to combine 'Fit & Healthy'? No, I don't think that's cheating, and given I picked Honesty and Integrity, clearly I would not cheat. Ha! I think Integrity incorporates Honesty. Down to 15. This is crazy. I will come back to this tomorrow.

~

Righto. I'm back. Heeeeere's ALICE! I am focussed (oh shit, does that mean I go up to 16? No, Focussed is not a core Value, just a state of mind for right now). Here is where I am:

Adventurous	*Independent*	*Financially secure*
Successful	*Ethical*	*Well-regarded*
Professional	*Integrity*	*Respected*
Competitive	*Family-oriented*	*Fit & Healthy*
Empathetic	*Expert*	*Loving*

Lose Professional; Well-regarded is a hard one. Hmmm. Lose it.

Nup; put Professional back in. That's important.

Lose Competitive; Expert; Empathetic. Slashing and burning here.

Combine Integrity and Ethical? I think Integrity encapsulates Ethical. Lose Ethical.

That's it, I've got 10. Sue me.

Adventurous
Successful
Professional
Independent
Integrity
Family-oriented
Fit & Healthy
Loving
Financially secure
Respected

Trade-off time - prioritising your Top Values

In a minute you will prioritise your Top Values in the order of the most important to you to the least. But first, you need to understand that there will be trade-offs. You will have a long list of what you desire out of life for yourself, your partner, your children and the community in which you live. From time to time these desires will come into conflict with one another. When this occurs you need to make a choice. For example, if one of your Values is *Success at Work* (for instance, to reach the highest possible level in your career), while another is to be *Family-oriented* (say, to be present at all of your child's major school milestones), something will need to give. There will be a trade-off because you can't have both of these things all of the time at the same time.

— *What other women say* —

Amy Poynton, Business Advisor, Board Member (retired partner Ernst & Young)

I got my first job when I was 14. I have always worked. I always expected that there would be trade-offs. I expected to be able to have access to it all, but I never expected to have it stitched up and completely balanced. There are always trade-offs.

Janine Allis, Founder and Managing Director Boost Juice (Retail Zoo)

It's about priorities. I don't care if the house is tidy. If I have spare time, I'd rather close the door on the mess and take the kids to the park.

Your Top Values are the measures you use consciously or not to assess whether you are really living the life you want to live. More importantly, for the purposes of getting back 30 hours a month:

- they will help you see whether you are spending your time on what you want to spend your time on; and
- they will make it much easier for you to discard the stuff that just does not float your boat.

In prioritising your Top Values the concept of trade-offs can be confronting, and frankly, from time to time, upsetting. Your instinct might be to put your family as your top priority just because you think you should. Don't fall for this trap. To help list your priorities properly, think about the trade-offs you make each and every day, as these are the decisions that reflect your true Values. If you love your career and work hard at it, but generally sacrifice events involving your kids (such a school sports days), then reflect on what that means in terms of the order of what you value most.

This is not a list of who you love most. In short, be honest with yourself - this is about living your life smarter and no-one is here to judge you.

— *What other women say* —

Janine Allis, Founder and Managing Director Boost Juice (Retail Zoo)

I could have looked after myself better. But I have actually loved this journey. It has been the ultimate in self-development.

Amy Poynton, Business Advisor, Board Member (retired partner Ernst & Young)

It's easy to get your priorities mixed up. I remember a day when I received a call at work to collect my sick son from crèche. I had only recently joined the company and I was in the middle of something important at work. I had no-one else who could collect my son. I was building my career and I made the decision to put work first – I told the crèche I would get there as soon as I could. When I arrived at the crèche 2 hours later, my son was really sick.

I had made the wrong choice and that decision marked me. It knocked my priorities back into place. I still feel ill when I think about it. But in resetting my priorities I put in place proper plans for next time an emergency arose. With my next employer I made it clear that if I had a sick child I would need to leave work on occasion. They accepted that. They supported me. There was no guilt.

This type of trade-off is very common, and regardless of the decision you make, your choice will invariably bring with it guilt. Life deals us challenges and we need to steer a course which represents a reasonable and fair balance.

Exercise 4 - Prioritising My Top Values

Write your Values onto sticky notes. Spread them out and sort them into three piles. The ones which are obviously your highest should be easy. Move them to the left. Then pull out the ones which you feel are definitely lower down and move them right. What remains are your mid-range Values. Put each of the smaller piles into order of most important to least, then combine them into one list.

My Top Values in order of priority are:

◇◇

Alice's Me Time Diary

God, this is hard. I feel like I should say Family-oriented is my Number One but in all honesty I think that success at work is up there too. I mean, look at all the work values I had on my original list of 25!

But, if I had to choose between spending 5 hours winning a great new client and getting that buzz of success OR spending 5 hours watching a dance recital to see Olive in one 5-minute dance, I am choosing the work. Every single time. It's an absolute no-brainer. That doesn't mean I don't love Olive more than life itself, it just means that I would rather poke my eye out with a blunt stick than watch a 5-hour dance recital.

True.

OK. Now I feel like a bad mum. The guilt is kicking in.

No, I'm not a bad mum! I'm just being honest. There is plenty I love about being a mum. Just not dance recitals. Success is important to me. God, just get over it Alice.

1. Successful	*4. Loving*	*7. Adventurous*
2. Family-oriented	*5. Ethical & Integrity*	*8. Respected*
3. Fit & Healthy	*6. Financially secure*	*9. Independent*

OK, good. Finally decided to get rid of 'Professional', it doesn't feel as strong as the other values. Down to 9. That will do. I have 9 Values.

I actually feel pretty good about my list.

◇◇

Nice Work. Now You Know:

- Your personal pain points, or time management challenges
- How you are feeling right now
- Your Values and their order of priority - the things in life which are most important to you and to your sense of wellbeing.

It's Time to MAP your time.

STEP 2: MAP

Ask most people and they won't be fully aware of where their time goes. This isn't unusual. But how can you expect to start managing your time smarter, including getting rid of time wasting habits, until you know where you are currently spending your time?

In order to understand where you are today and where you want to be, by the end of Step 2 Map you will have:

- A map of your Standard Day in detail
- A map of your Dream Day in detail

Hello? Hello? Where did you go ...?

Alice's Me Time Diary

So, I have this book - Me Time. I'm supposed to get back 30 hours of lost time a month. Yeah right. There is no way I can find 30 extra hours a month. No way. I know for a fact that I am busier than a blue-arsed fly. I am up early and I keep going until it's late. Go, go, go. I'm like one of those intense mechanical bunnies you see on TV.

But it would be nice to have an extra 30 hours a month. Hell, that's ... hang on, let me get my calculator ... 360 extra hours a year! Who would have thought I would need a calculator to add that one up?

Maybe I should give this a proper go. Because, in all honesty, there just aren't enough hours in my day to get it all done.

OK, so what exactly do I do all day? If I track my time in detail, I guess I'll see the stuff which is a waste of my time, and then I can get rid of it? Is that the process? Plus it would be good to get an idea of what I need to do, what I don't need to do and what I can do better, quicker or smarter.

I know what I need to stop doing - checking Facebook and searching for old boyfriends or girls I disliked at school. Not a good use of my time. But rewarding, especially when they have gone to pasture and have lost their hair (the ex-boyfriends not the girls). However a good balding gal can bring a smile to my face too ...

And yet I diverge. Distractions, clearly another time-wasting problem for me.

I am very good at multi-tasking. Really, I am. Few can whip up a stir fry while coming up with 3 reasons why Australia should be a Republic while running the vacuum over the spilt noodles. I am 'the' champion of multi-tasking.

But I do get a bit bogged down on emails. I pop in and out of those damned messages every time I hear a ping from my computer. Why do I do this? Got to stop the compulsive email thing.

I am bloody good at sitting down and focussing on managing my clients. I love it, it energises me. I get lots done when I'm in pure work mode.

What should I make for dinner tonight? Maybe spaghetti bolognaise. I have everything I need. Oh damn it, no mince. I need to run down to the supermarket to grab some mince. Need milk too.

[Ping] ... a new email!

◇◇

Every single day seems to be as full and demanding as the one before. It never, ever stops. You never, ever stop. You manage your home, your family, your career or business, your team and your down time (your what?). And with being constantly accessible via technology you don't often switch off until you fall into bed each night. Hand up if you take your phone to bed with you, and then occasionally send an email or text after midnight?

But do you actually know what you do all day as you busily buzz about like that blue-arsed fly? Because if you don't know where you spend your time, in detail, you won't know what you need to change. I would love $1 for every time someone says that their day *literally* flies by and that there is not actually a lot of time between 8am and 6pm. Really?

You need to map your time. Grab a cup of tea and settle in, because this exercise needs your true focus.

Exercise - My Standard Day

Purpose

Monitoring where you currently spend your time is central to improving how you manage your time. This involves recording what you do over a given period. There is a week's worth of Time Sheets (including Saturday and Sunday) in the *Me Time* Workbook. Below is an extract of the Time Sheets which will allow you to record how you spend one Standard Day (for the purposes of this exercise, Alice has also only completed one day).

You need to complete the whole week - doing the extra work will definitely maximise the number of lost hours you identify. This process is also useful as obviously not every day will map out the same.

So that you don't miss anything, think about your time across the major areas where you spend your life:

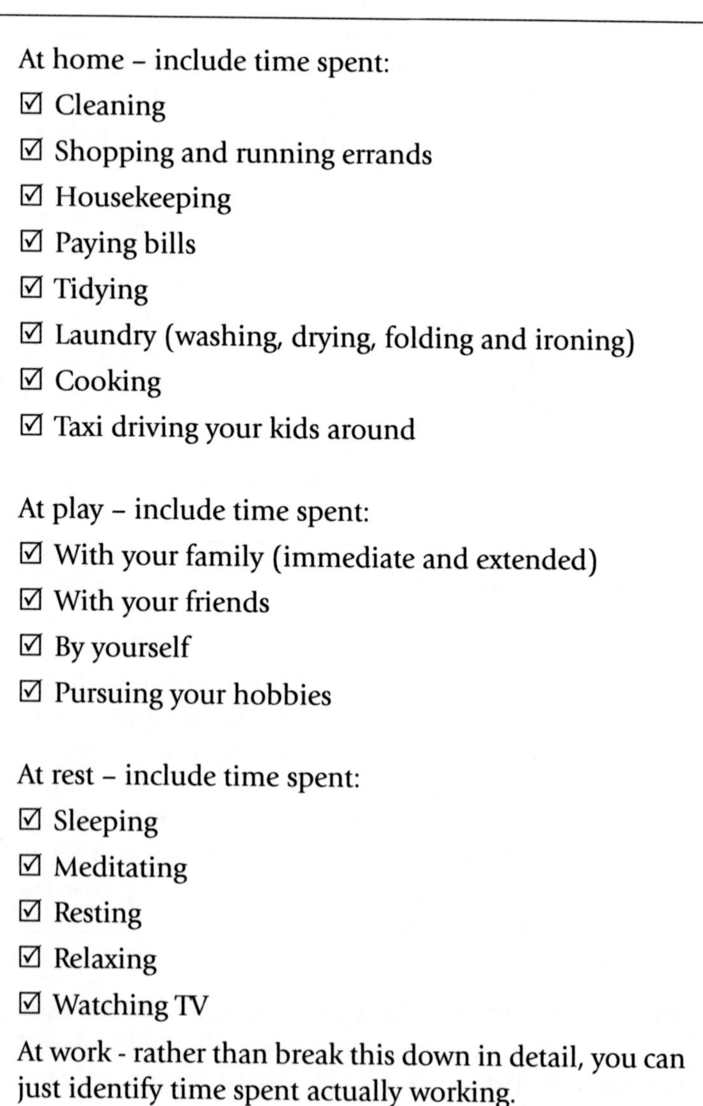

At home – include time spent:

- ☑ Cleaning
- ☑ Shopping and running errands
- ☑ Housekeeping
- ☑ Paying bills
- ☑ Tidying
- ☑ Laundry (washing, drying, folding and ironing)
- ☑ Cooking
- ☑ Taxi driving your kids around

At play – include time spent:

- ☑ With your family (immediate and extended)
- ☑ With your friends
- ☑ By yourself
- ☑ Pursuing your hobbies

At rest – include time spent:

- ☑ Sleeping
- ☑ Meditating
- ☑ Resting
- ☑ Relaxing
- ☑ Watching TV

At work - rather than break this down in detail, you can just identify time spent actually working.

Actions:

- Take some time to capture what you do on a Standard (or average) Day and identify the time spent on each task. At this stage you only need to complete Column 1. You will return to the other columns in future Steps.
- Include everything you do on a typical day - from getting up, making breakfast, showering and getting dressed, travelling time, Facebook time, work, doing the dishes, washing the clothes, supermarket trips, making meals, eating meals, cleaning, tidying, telephone calls, and so on. You get the picture.
- Estimate the amount of time you spend on each task as this will help you achieve better results in the long run. Don't underestimate your time or write down what time you wish you had spent on a task.
- Be honest - if you know you spend an hour on Facebook before you get down to work then write it down. Now is not the time to fudge the data. You will get your best results from being honest with yourself.
- This is not a test. No-one is judging you. No-one is even going to see this stuff. But if you are skiving off for a quick romp with the postman each afternoon then maybe be creative with your task descriptions just in case - *Collecting the post* will do the trick.

My Standard Day - Time Sheet

	Column 1	Column 2	Column 3	Column 4
Time spent	Weekday	Must/Want/ Delegate/ Reject	$ Spend	Costs
5-6am				
6-7am				
7-8am				
8-9am				
9-10am				
10-11am				
11-12noon				
noon-1pm				
1-2pm				
2-3pm				
3-4pm				
4-5pm				
5-6pm				
6-7pm				
7-8pm				
8-9pm				
9-10pm				
10-11pm				
11-12mn				
12-1am				

Alice's Me Time Diary

	Column 1
Time spent	Weekday
5-6am	*Sleep*
6-7am	*Get up* *30 min jog* *10 min shower, including wiping down shower* *10 min make brekky for myself and kids* *5 min eat brekky* *5 min stand in front of fridge and make mental shopping list*
7-8am	*10 min make kids lunches* *10 min tidy up after everyone's brekky* *10 min find Henry's sports clothes* *5 min nag kids to brush teeth* *15 min get dressed and throw on some makeup* *5 min pack my bag* *5 min yelling at kids to hurry up*
8-9am	*10 min drive kids to school and do the drop-and-run* *30 min drive into town, making work calls* *5 min park car and walk to office building* *10 min grab takeaway coffee* *5 min hellos as I walk to my office*
9-10am	*10 min check emails* *10 min on Facebook - networking right?* *40 min work*
10-11am	*60 min work*
11-12noon	*60 min work*
noon-1pm	*15 min grab some sushi* *20 min at supermarket grabbing essentials for tonight* *15 eating sushi while checking Facebook* *10 min make cup of coffee and chat*
1-2pm	*60 min work*
2-3pm	*5 min fresh air* *5 min chat to John on the phone* *50 min work*
3-4pm	*60 min work*

4-5pm	*55 min work* *5 min dash to the car*
5-6pm	*30 min drive to school to collect kids, making work calls* *5 min drive kids to after-school activities, making work calls. Drop Olive at dance class (there is no way I am going to stay and watch!) and Henry at basketball* *25 min dash home and clean kitchen, chuck some chemicals down the toilet and give a quick brush and flush, stand in front of fridge again thinking about what I need*
6-7pm	*5 min bring in washing and pour washing on to yesterday's pile of washing* *20 min start dinner* *5 min pick kids up from activities* *5 min get kids set up with homework* *15 min start folding washing, help with homework, turn on bath, put chickens away and collect eggs, feed cat* *10 min keep an eye on dinner and tidy up kitchen, working like a maniac here*
7-8pm	*15 min get kids in bath, finish dinner prep, tidying as I go, set table* *20 min get kids out of bath, yell at them to stop fighting, yell at them to get into their PJs, yell at them to put their homework away, put their homework away myself, yell at them to get their lunch boxes out of their bags, get the lunch boxes out of their bags myself, yell at them to put their folded clothes away, do that myself too.* *25 min eat dinner*
8-9pm	*20 min read with kids while John clearing table and loading dishwasher* *10 min cuddle kids and put them to bed, try not to fall asleep myself* *20 min talk with John. Who? Oh yes, I remember you. My husband* *10 min vacuum kitchen floor, finish the dishes, put leftovers away*
9-10pm	*15 min tidy up all the kids' crap* *20 min check Facebook* *10 min check diary for tomorrow* *Fall asleep on couch*
10-11pm	*sleeping*
11-12mn	*sleeping*
12-1am	*sleeping*

Reminder: this only shows one day, but your task is to map an entire week, including the weekends.

◇◇

Huh?

Looking over your Standard Day can be daunting. The first thing you might think is, *Wow I do a lot!* and you might even think, *Wow I spend a lot of my time on a whole lot of crap!*

But, the important thing at this stage of the process is not to judge yourself. The whole point of reading *Me Time* is to get back 30 hours a month to live the life you want. You wouldn't be reading *Me Time* if you didn't want to change. You wouldn't be reading *Me Time* if you were already living the life that you wanted. You are reading *Me Time* because you WANT MORE TIME (and some help in getting there).

I mean, where did you actually think your extra 30 hours were going to come from? It's not magic. Obviously the time you get back at the end of *Me Time* will come from reworking the time you already have. So stick with me and let's get on with it.

Now, for a change of pace let's consider your Dream Day.

Exercise - My Dream Day

Purpose

To imagine how different things could be - to see exactly what your best day ever would look like.

How would a Dream Day pan out for you? Not the dream day where you swim with Brad Pitt on a private beach in Bali. This is about the Dream Day you spend if your Standard Day just got a whole lot better.

Fill out the Dream Day Time Sheet below capturing your own personal Dream Day.

Actions:

- Only include the things which would make your day better - from a half hour sleep in; breakfast in bed; how long you take to get ready; sitting down at your desk without procrastinating and working in a goal-oriented way through your emails in record time; followed by time to spend on your new strategy for growth in your business; a few meetings; coming home to a clean house; washing has been done; meal is prepared; time for a soothing bath before spending time with your family.
- Again - no-one is looking over your shoulder here. Be honest and tell it like it is.

My Dream Day - Time Sheet

Time Spent	My Dream Day
5-6am	
6-7am	
7-8am	
8-9am	
9-10am	
10-11am	
11-12noon	
noon-1pm	
1-2pm	
2-3pm	
3-4pm	

4-5pm	
5-6pm	
6-7pm	
7-8pm	
8-9pm	
9-10pm	
10-11pm	
11-12mn	
12-1am	

Alice's Me Time Diary

Time Spent	My Dream Day
5-6am	*Sleeping peacefully after not waking or stirring once, no-one had a nightmare, no-one had a temperature, John didn't snore. Wake feeling extraordinarily refreshed. Who is this woman?*
6-7am	*30 min jog with John (snort) and feel even better!* *10 min shower, but no need to wipe it down as it's already clean* *Kids are already up & they have made, eaten and put away their own brekky & loaded the dishwasher (hahaha!).* *20 min make my own brekky, eat it in peace, kids get themselves organised without whinging.*
7-8am	*No need to make kids lunches as it's 'Teachers Make the Lunch Day' today – yay!* *25 min get dressed, put on some proper makeup. Kids tell me how nice I look. John says I am one red hot sexy woman. Brad Pitt calls – oh, no, sorry forgot it's Dream Day not Fantasy Day.* *35 min – ummm. Spare time. Chat to John.*

8-9am	*Kids want to ride their bikes to school, together, on their own, without me. No tears, no drama, no fights. They even appear to like each other.* *5 min wave kids off and smile lovingly at the candid camera, as surely there must be one hiding there in the bushes.* *15 min drive to work because there is no traffic.* *5 min park car.* *30 min morning meeting in the coffee shop.* *5 min cleaner calls to see if I would like him to prepare dinner tonight. Um, yes please.*
9-3pm	*Awesomely efficient @ work, so much so that I pop out for an hour to meet John for lunch in town. OMG it's a day date!*
3-4pm	*5 min get car & leave work early.* *15 min drive home - no traffic. Arrive home @ the same time as the kids.* *40 min make afternoon tea with the kids, spend quality time with them talking about their day & they remember what they did & they answer me in full sentences. No-one wants the TV on. Everyone is happy and smiling, because we are a happy, smiling, non-TV watching, blissfully beautiful family where everyone is kind, considerate & encouraging of each other.* *Feeling relaxed & enjoying the company of my kids.* *The house has been cleaned to within an inch of its life and dinner is prepared.* *Kids promise not to mess it up the house – & they don't!* *John arrives home early, with flowers.*
4-5pm	*30 min drive kids to after-school activities & decide not to just drop-and-run, and stay & watch. Kids thrilled. Catch up with other parents.* *5 min cleaner calls and reminds me I don't need to go to the supermarket because he shopped for us today. Bless him.* *5 min drive home from activities.* *20 min kids do their homework with John so I go for a walk with the dog. Dog delighted.*
5-6pm	*Kids have done their homework & they tidy it away!* *20 min kids feed pets & play in the backyard. Reminds me of my childhood.* *40 min John & I enjoy a G&T & chat about our day. Kids don't interrupt.*
6-7pm	*60 min eat dinner all together & share great conversation with the kids – we are just like those families you see on TV!*
7-8pm	*60 min kids clear dinner away, load dishwasher, tidy the kitchen, put chickens away, run their own bath, hang up their own towels so I can sit and chill with John, again. Hello John!*
8-9pm	*60 min we play a family board game. I swear to God I am not kidding.*
9-10pm	*20 min kids go to bed without any fuss, read to me while John cleans up.* *40 min John and I watch our favourite TV show.*
10-11pm	*I stay up later than usual because I am not dog tired. John & I even have the strength & desire to head to the boudoir (Dream Day, right?).*

You have mapped out your Standard Day(s) and your wonderful Dream Day. Take a few minutes to compare your Standard Day to your Dream Day. Apart from the fact that your Dream Day looks a whole lot better, which of the following statements resonate most strongly with you:

Exercise - What Do I Think?

Purpose

To get a little perspective - how far away from your Dream Day are you?

My Standard Day looks:	My Dream Day looks:
Worse than I thought	Bloody awesome
Overwhelming	A whole less cluttered
Crazy	More rewarding
Unsustainable	Less stressful
Help me	More challenging
Not too bad, I am a busy lady	Worth striving for
Like it should, this is life	Beyond my reach
	Completely unrealistic
	Unattainable
	A fast track to feeling guilty
	What it is, 'a Dream'

Alice's Me Time Diary

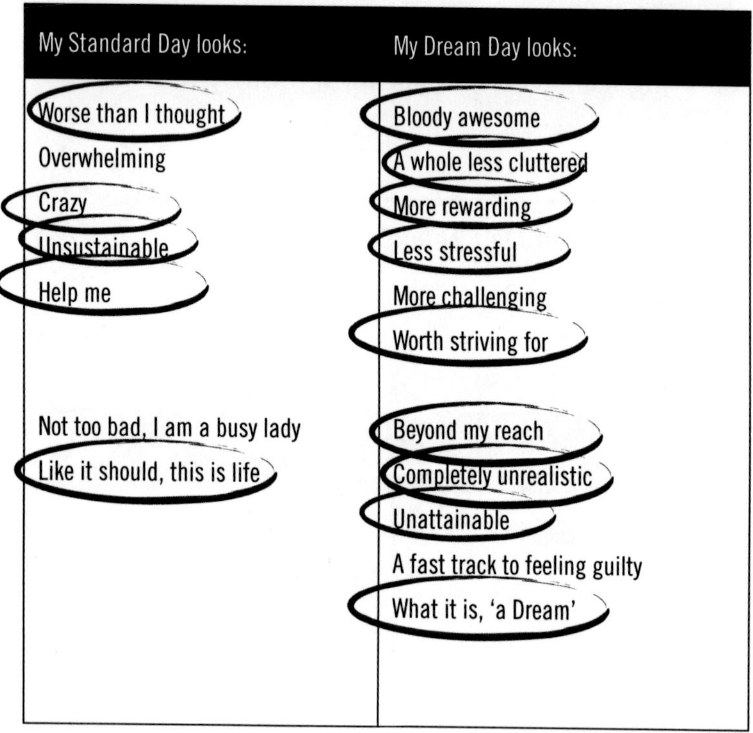

My Standard Day looks:	My Dream Day looks:
Worse than I thought	Bloody awesome
Overwhelming	A whole less cluttered
Crazy	More rewarding
Unsustainable	Less stressful
Help me	More challenging
	Worth striving for
Not too bad, I am a busy lady	Beyond my reach
Like it should, this is life	Completely unrealistic
	Unattainable
	A fast track to feeling guilty
	What it is, 'a Dream'

Many of you will have circled more than a few of the statements above - even the negative comments about your Dream Day. This is completely normal. While you can see that your Dream Day looks absolutely fabulous, it is also a little hard at this point in time to see how you are going to get from A to B.

Don't worry - remember it's a process and you are right on track.

Nice Work. Now You Know:

- Exactly where all of your time goes each day. You will come back to this throughout *Me Time* because you will continue to identify additional forgotten chores or lost pieces of time that you can add to your Standard Day.
- You know what your Dream Day looks like and this is what you are working towards. Yes it is a Dream, but even if you got halfway there that's 50% better than the way you are living right now. Yes?

It's time to ANALYSE your Standard Day to find those hours of lost time.

STEP 3: ANALYSE

When it comes to managing your time smarter, and getting back 30 hours a month, it is key to analyse and categorise your time. Analysing and categorising your time will give you a much clearer picture of exactly what you do each day, and importantly, provide insight into what you can let go, and what you can start doing a whole lot smarter.

Alice's Me Time Diary

I don't actually think I am that bad when it comes to managing my time. I know I have my bad days, but on the whole I am a successful woman - I get stuff done. Just look at my Standard Day - I couldn't jam another thing in!

Oh yeah, right, that's not actually a good thing here. That's like proving I am the best at being stupidly busy.

I guess I have always been the Go To girl - 'give it to Alice because it will get done' is what they say. That's just how I rock, and I guess I like it. But that's no longer the right answer. In fact, that's half the problem.

I do wonder ... my Dream Day looked blissful. Maybe I will print it out and keep it close.

Is it achievable? It had better be!

Break it down Baby

In categorising your time, focus on your Standard Day and divide your time into the following four distinct Time Segments:

Time Segment	Explanation	Examples
MUSTs	There are a core set of Musts that every human has and there are your own set of personal Musts. Generally speaking, the latter is the stuff that you have to do because only you can do it.	• Eat • Sleep • Work/earn • Mentor the young person in your work group
WANTs	This is the stuff that you would love to do and that you will soon be doing a whole lot more of when you get back 30 hours a month.	• Exercise • Read • Garden • Cook • Massage • Family time
DELEGATEs	This is the stuff that you are currently doing but which can easily be done for you by someone else. This list is fairly universal, but depending on just how much you actually do, your list could be pretty long.	• Cooking dinner • Tidying up • Cleaning the house • Loading/unloading the dishwasher • Walking the dog • Doing the shopping • Hanging up the wet towels again and again • Washing/ironing • Mum's taxi ... and so on

REJECTs	This is the stuff that no-one really needs to do or which you could do a whole lot smarter. This is the absolute gold of wasted time.	• Washing clothes that aren't dirty • 5 trips to the supermarket a week • Slaving to your partner/children

Exercises

Purpose

There are 5 exercises below. Their purpose is to help you:

- Reflect on the four Time Segments above and consider how you spend your time each day
- Identify the tasks you Must do, those you Want to do, what you can Delegate, and what you can Reject
- Quantify how much time you are spending each day on each of the 4 Time Segments.

Exercise 1 - Musts and Wants

Actions:

- Go back to your *Me Time* Workbook and get out the Standard Day Time Sheet/s where you have completed Column 1.
- Complete Column 2 and identify each task you clearly consider to be something you Must do or something you Want to do. This should be fairly easy to do.
- If a task doesn't feel like a Must or a Want, leave a

blank next to it - it will most likely be either a Delegate or Reject, which will be addressed in Exercise 2 below.

- You may feel that there is an overlap between Musts and Wants for a given task - for example, working and making money could well be a Must (you have to earn a living right?) but also a Want (with any luck you absolutely love what you do). Where there is an overlap, allocate the task to one Time Segment only - weigh it up and select the Time Segment that intuitively seems to have the stronger pull for you.
- Equally, there will be some tasks which you might feel obliged to allocate to a Must or Want by virtue of pure guilt (go back to *Judgement Time* if you need a reminder about guilt). This is a trap. Be honest. If you dread a task then that's a pretty good indication that it isn't really a Must or a Want.

You now have a clear idea of the tasks that you Must do and those that you Want to do. Classifying your Delegates and Rejects can be a little harder, but you are on a roll, so let's push on.

Exercise 2 - Delegates and Rejects

Actions:

- Absolute honesty is key.
- When it comes to Delegates, think of the tasks which:
  - can be done by someone else who you don't have to pay (e.g., a partner, child, grandparent). For example, your partner is quite capable of cooking the occasional dinner. Kids from the age of 3 are

definitely capable of clearing the dinner table. Kids who are 6 and older are happily capable of a whole lot more; or

- can be done by someone else who you do need to pay (e.g., hired domestic help).

- Just because you identify a task as something that you might be able to Delegate, does not mean you have to Delegate it. Just circle it for now as a potential task for delegation - we will get to the actual process of delegation later.
- When it comes to Rejects, think of the tasks in your Standard Day which you know that you can do better. For example, if you are (like I used to be) one of those clever women who decides what to make for dinner somewhere around 3pm each day and then heads to the supermarket and buys what you need to make that dinner on the way home from work, it might surprise you to know that this is not the most efficient use of your time. Circle it. There is a better way.
- This is an iterative process. You will come back to your Standard Day in the next Steps as you become clearer on your Musts, Wants, Delegates and Rejects.

Alice's Me Time Diary

	Column 1	Column 2
Time spent	Weekday	Must/Want/ Delegate/Reject
5-6am	*Sleep*	
6-7am	*Get up* *30 min jog* *10 min shower, including wiping down shower* *10 min make brekky for myself and kids* *5 min eat brekky* *5 min stand in front of fridge and make mental shopping list*	*Must* *Want* *Must* *Must* *Must* *Reject*
7-8am	*10 min make kids lunches* *10 min tidy up after everyone's brekky* *10 min find Henry's sports clothes* *5 min nag kids to brush teeth* *15 min get dressed and throw on some makeup* *5 min pack my bag* *5 min yelling at kids to hurry up*	*Must* *Must* *Must* *Reject* *Must* *Must* *Reject*
8-9am	*10 min drive kids to school and do the drop-and-run* *30 min drive into town, making work calls* *5 min park car and walk to office building* *10 min grab takeaway coffee* *5 min hellos as I walk to my office*	*Must* *Must* *Must* *Want* *Want*
9-10am	*10 min check emails* *10 min on Facebook - networking right?* *40 min work*	*Must* *Must* *Must*
10-11am	*60 min work*	*Must*
11-12noon	*60 min work*	*Must*
noon-1pm	*15 min grab some sushi* *20 min at supermarket grabbing essentials for tonight* *15 eating sushi while checking Facebook* *10 min make cup of coffee and chat*	*Want* *Must* *Must* *Want*
1-2pm	*60 min work*	*Must*
2-3pm	*5 min fresh air* *5 min chat to John on the phone* *50 min work*	*Want* *Want* *Must*
3-4pm	*60 min work*	*Must*

4-5pm	*55 min work* *5 min dash to the car*	*Must* *Must*
5-6pm	*30 min drive to school to collect kids, making work calls* *5 min drive kids to after-school activities, making work calls. Drop Olive at dance class (there is no way I am going to stay and watch!) and Henry at basketball* *25 min dash home and clean kitchen, chuck some chemicals down the toilet and give a quick brush and flu sh, stand in front of fridge again thinking about what I need*	*Must* *Must* *Must*
6-7pm	*5 min bring in washing and pour washing on to yesterday's pile of washing* *20 min start dinner* *5 min pick kids up from activities* *5 min get kids set up with homework* *15 min start folding washing, help with homework, turn on bath, put chickens away and collect eggs, feed cat* *10 min keep an eye on dinner and tidy up kitchen, working like a maniac here*	*Must* *Must* *Must* *Must* *Delegate* *Must*
7-8pm	*15 min get kids in bath, finish dinner prep, tidying as I go, set table* *20 min get kids out of bath, yell at them to stop fighting, yell at them to get into their PJs, yell at them to put their homework away, put their homework away myself, yell at them to get their lunch boxes out of their bags, get the lunch boxes out of their bags myself, yell at them to put their folded clothes away, do that myself too.* *25 min eat dinner*	*Must* *Delegate* *Must*
8-9pm	*20 min read with kids while John clearing table and loading dishwasher* *10 min cuddle kids and put them to bed, try not to fall asleep myself* *20 min talk with John. Who? Oh yes, I remember you. My husband* *10 min vacuum kitchen floor, finish the dishes, put leftovers away*	*Want* *Want* *Want* *Must*
9-10pm	*15 min tidy up all the kids' crap* *20 min check Facebook* *10 min check diary for tomorrow* *Fall asleep on couch*	*Delegate* *Reject* *Must* *Reject*

I need to eat - so that's a Must.

Family time and eating dinner together every night - Want.

The cleaning tasks - Delegate.

I don't like watching Olive at dance class - I really don't want to do it. It's a Reject. Ouch. Maybe Mum can do it - Delegate? Now I feel bad.

I'm wasting time faffing about on Facebook. I thought it was a good way to grow my network for work, but clearly I have not been doing this strategically. I have been resorting to Facebook when I need a break from work but I am getting stuck there. (sigh) Reject? hmmmm ...

I am a great mum but I have somehow become my kids' slave. I am going crazy tidying up after the kids every day, it does my head in. It's a Delegate. They really are old enough to be doing some of this stuff themselves. John too - surely?

I love my job. Must/Want/Must/Want. Make it a Must for now - my real need is to earn money.

I don't do much for myself. Jogging is definitely a Want.

There is a lot here I don't want to do. Why am I doing it?

◇◇

Exercise 3 - My First Time Cut

Actions:

- With Columns 1 and 2 of your Standard Day now complete, add up the total time you spend on each of the 4 Time Segments.
- The time allocation does not need to be recorded down to the last millisecond (in all of Alice's tables she rounds up or down to make the calculations easier). All you want is a reasonable estimate of the time you spend on each task - use Alice's table and her thought process at Exercise 2 above as a guide.
- Write your total time spend down here:

Musts	Wants	Delegates	Rejects

◇◇

Alice's Me Time Diary

Musts	Wants	Delegates	Rejects
12 hours 15 mins	2 hours 10 min	50 min	35 min

◇◇

Having undertaken the first cut of your time in your Standard Day, it's helpful to have a look at the time you will save if you put in place each and every one of the Delegates and Rejects you have identified so far.

Exercise 4 - How many Hours could I Save?

Action:

- Remember, this is just your first cut and nothing is set in concrete - the hours you save will change as you continue to work through the *5 Steps to Being SMART*. But it is nice to see that there is good, solid time you can get back!

		Total
A	The number of hours I will save each day if I delegate everything in my Delegate list	
B	The number of hours I will save each day if I discard or better manage everything in my Rejects list	
C	(A + B) x 30 days = the number of hours I can get back a month	

◇◇

Alice's Me Time Diary

		Total
A	The number of hours I will save each day if I delegate everything in my Delegate list	*50 min*
B	The number of hours I will save each day if I discard or better manage everything in my Rejects list	*35 min*
C	(A + B) x 30 days = the number of hours I can get back a month *(50 + 35) = 85 mins x 30 = 2550 mins = 42 hours 30 mins*	*42 hours 30 mins*

Really? Wow!

◇◇

Awesome! Yes?

Fold down the corner of page 92. This stuff is gold and you are going to want to come back to this page again - especially if you ever feel that you need a little motivation.

What is this costing you?

You have a great career or a great business and you have come this far by yourself based on talent and lots of hard work. But time is short. You have already seen from your Standard Day that your schedule is pretty full. There is no room for more. And it doesn't matter how talented you are, if you don't have any time left to give, how can you take yourself to the next step in your career or the next growth stage in your business? Your current time management behaviours represent a big threat to your ongoing success.

How so? Well, let's analyse what your time management habits are costing you. You need to look at your time differently to see where you are losing productivity and a whole lot more.

> ***If you are currently using your time really well, you will at least lift the bar even higher.***

An effective use of your time is where the vast majority of your time is spent on your Musts and Wants. Most likely, however, what you have discovered in getting this far is that the way you currently use your time is not always the best use of your time.

And just what is this costing you? Probably, a whole lot more than you thought.

Not all time is created equal

When it comes to time - not all time is created equal. Yes, it is true that we all have the same 24 hours and every hour has 60 minutes and every minute has 60 seconds. But each hour is very different from the one before and, more importantly, how you allocate, manage and then use your time in each of those hours will be very different.

— *What other women say* —

Tanya McVicar, Head of Operational Risk & Compliance, Personal Banking at National Australia Bank

By sitting down and working out what my time is actually worth, it helped me focus on which use of my time I value most. Seeing the dollars in black and white made the efficient management of my time even more crucial.

For example, I know that allocating an hour contributing to the strategic growth of the Personal Bank is something I value, but how I then manage that hour will impact on my sense of achievement. Let me explain. If I schedule an hour for strategy and I spend that time without interruption and with complete focus, then I know that I have really valued my time and used it well. However, if I allocate an hour for strategy, and then interruptions arise which take my focus, and then I stare out the window and procrastinate a little, and then I flick through my emails and become even more distracted, and then I take a number of phone calls, all before coming back to the strategic plan, I have wasted a perfectly good hour.

I have used two hours of my time, but that time was not equal. The first hour was a highly efficient use of my time, the second was rubbish. And I feel that waste. I have not valued my own time.

Don't take a guess at what your time management habits are costing you. You want the facts. You need to work out exactly what your time is worth. Knowing what your time is worth will:

- motivate you to drive some different time management habits
- help you realise the true value of your time, and
- help you decide whether any given job or task is the best use of your time.

Costing out your time in 3 different ways will allow you to look at how you spend your time through different lenses - one might resonate more strongly with you than the others.

Just to reiterate: not all time is created equal. Some tasks, such as choosing to watch your kids play sport instead of spending an hour at work may not be the best use of your time productively, however you may get enormous emotional wellbeing from your decision. Other tasks, such as vacuuming your house when you have a sore back might result in a clean floor, but it is not necessarily the best use of your time physically.

The three cost lenses

You have 24 hours a day and you make choices about how you spend that time. Your choices will be influenced by:

Cost lens	Explanation	Example
Opportunity Cost	Each time you are presented with different options and you make a choice, there is a value you place on that choice. The opportunity cost of your choice is what you gave up to get it.	You choose to spend an hour of your time with your kids rather than at the gym.

	If you choose one task over another task, what is the opportunity or cost benefit of making one choice over the other?	Your opportunity cost is your workout.
Emotional Cost	Sometimes when you make a choice there will be an emotional cost associated with your decision. How do you feel when you spend your time well, or when you don't? What are your current time habits costing you emotionally?	You travel to New York for work and on arrival you learn that your son has broken his leg. Your husband tells you to stay in New York, and you do. Your emotional cost is guilt.
Physical Cost	Sometimes when you make a choice there will be a physical cost associated with your decision. How are you physically holding up by spending your time in this way? What are your current time habits costing you physically?	Rather than wait for help, you decide to move the coffee table yourself and you hurt your shoulder. You are in agony for a week. Your physical cost is pain and recovery time.

Opportunity Cost - time is money

The Opportunity Cost of how we use our time is generally a very compelling influence on how we choose to spend our time. If this is the case for you, then let's look at what your time is worth and what your Opportunity Costs are.

Exercises

Purpose

There are 3 exercises below which will demonstrate to you what your time is worth, in financial (dollar) terms, and then in terms of your Opportunity Cost.

Exercise 1 - My Hourly rate

If you know your hourly rate, your task is easy - just write down what you charge your clients for an hour of your time or what your employer pays you per hour if you are salaried:

My hourly rate is $..........

If you don't know your hourly rate, a quick way to calculate a sufficiently accurate hourly rate is to look at your most recent tax return and divide your taxable income (excluding interest and dividends) by 2,600 (this is the number of hours in a year you work if you generally work a 50 hour week), then round to the nearest dollar to make life simpler.

My annual Taxable Income is $............... divided by 2,600 = my hourly rate of $..............

Alice's Me Time Diary

My annual Taxable Income is $...$181,000... divided by 2,600 = my hourly rate of $...$70.00...

Exercise 2 - Costing my Standard Day

Actions:

- Go back to your Standard Day Time Sheet/s where you have completed Columns 1 and 2.
- It's time to fill in Column 3, noting down the financial cost against each task you perform based on your hourly rate. Do this by dividing your hourly rate by the amount of time each task takes you. For example, if your hourly rate is $70 and a task takes 30 minutes, then note down $35 against that task. Remember, use rounding to make life simpler.

Alice's Me Time Diary

	Column 1	Column 2	Column 3
Time spent	Weekday	Must/Want/ Delegate/Reject	$ Spend*
5-6am	*Sleep*	*Must*	
6-7am	*Get up* *30 min jog* *10 min shower, including wiping down shower* *10 min make brekky for myself and kids* *5 min eat brekky* *5 min stand in front of fridge and make mental shopping list*	*Must* *Want* *Must* *Must* *Must* *Reject*	 *$35* *$12* *$12* *$6* *$6*
7-8am	*10 min make kids lunches* *10 min tidy up after everyone's brekky* *10 min find Henry's sports clothes* *5 min nag kids to brush teeth* *15 min get dressed and throw on some makeup* *5 min pack my bag* *5 min yelling at kids to hurry up*	*Must* *Must* *Must* *Reject* *Must* *Must* *Reject*	*$12* *$12* *$12* *$6* *$18* *$6* *$6*
8-9am	*10 min drive kids to school and do the drop-and-run* *30 min drive into town, making work calls* *5 min park car and walk to office building* *10 min grab takeaway coffee* *5 min hellos as I walk to my office*	*Must* *Must* *Must* *Want* *Want*	*$12* *$35* *$6* *$12* *$6*
9-10am	*10 min check emails* *10 min on Facebook - networking right?* *40 min work*	*Must* *Must* *Must*	*$12* *$12* *$47*
10-11am	*60 min work*	*Must*	*$70*
11-12noon	*60 min work*	*Must*	*$70*
noon-1pm	*15 min grab some sushi* *20 min at supermarket grabbing essentials for tonight* *15 eating sushi while surfing internet* *10 min make cup of coffee and chat*	*Want* *Must* *Must* *Want*	*$18* *$23* *$18* *$12*
1-2pm	*60 min work*	*Must*	*$70*
2-3pm	*5 min fresh air* *5 min chat to John on the phone* *50 min work*	*Want* *Want* *Must*	*$6* *$6* *$58*
3-4pm	*60 min work*	*Must*	*$70*

4-5pm	*55 min work* *5 min dash to the car*	*Must* *Must*	*$64* *$6*
5-6pm	*30 min drive to school to collect kids, making work calls* *5 min drive kids to after-school activities, making work calls. Drop Olive at dance class (there is no way I am going to stay and watch!) and Henry at basketball* *25 min dash home and clean kitchen, chuck some chemicals down the toilet and give a quick brush and flush, stand in front of fridge again thinking about what I need*	*Must* *Must* *Must*	*$35* *$6* *$29*
6-7pm	*5 min bring in washing and pour washing on to yesterday's pile of washing* *20 min start dinner* *5 min pick kids up from activities* *5 min get kids set up with homework* *15 min start folding washing, help with homework, turn on bath, put chickens away and collect eggs, feed cat* *10 min keep an eye on dinner and tidy up kitchen, working like a maniac here*	*Must* *Must* *Must* *Must* *Delegate* *Must*	*$6* *$23* *$6* *$6* *$18* *$12*
7-8pm	*15 min get kids in bath, finish dinner prep, tidying as I go, set table* *20 min get kids out of bath, yell at them to stop fighting, yell at them to get into their PJs, yell at them to put their homework away, put their homework away myself, yell at them to get their lunch boxes out of their bags, get the lunch boxes out of their bags myself, yell at them to put their folded clothes away, do that myself too.* *25 min eat dinner*	*Must* *Delegate* *Must*	*$18* *$23* *$29*
8-9pm	*20 min read with kids while John clearing table and loading dishwasher* *10 min cuddle kids and put them to bed, try not to fall asleep myself* *20 min talk with John. Who? Oh yes, I remember you. My husband* *10 min vacuum kitchen floor, finish the dishes, put leftovers away*	*Want* *Want* *Want* *Must*	*$23* *$12* *$23* *$12*
9-10pm	*15 min tidy up all the kids' crap* *20 min check Facebook* *10 min check diary for tomorrow* *Fall asleep on couch*	*Delegate* *Reject* *Must* *Reject*	*$18* *$23* *$12*

**all figures rounded to keep it simple*

Exercise 3 - My total Financial Cost for each Time Segment

Action:

Summarise your total Financial Cost for each Time Segment.

My Total Financial Cost for each Time Segment		
	$ per day	$...... per annum (daily rate x 260 business days)
Musts	$............................	$............................
Wants	$............................	$............................
Delegates	$............................	$............................
Rejects	$............................	$............................

◇◇

Alice's Me Time Diary

My Total Financial Cost for each Time Segment		
	$ per day	$...... per annum (daily rate x 260 business days)
Musts	$ *$852*	$ *$221,520*
Wants	$ *$152*	$ *$39,520*
Delegates	$ *$59*	$ *$15,340*
Rejects	$ *$41*	$ *$10,660*

Oh dear. Far out. Wow. I'm speechless.

◇◇

Confronting? I hope so.

The above methodology gives a good approximation of what your time is worth and that you may, and most likely have, been spending many hours (and many dollars) performing tasks or chores that no-one would dream of paying you for.

> Alice, for example, is spending $41.00 of her time (35 minutes) a Standard Day on things she knows she can Delegate. That's $10,660.00 per annum at her hourly rate!

It gets even more challenging when you take this financial cost and add in your Opportunity Cost.

Opportunity Cost is associated with anything of value (financial or otherwise, such as a lost benefit or a lost pleasure) that you have to give up to acquire or achieve something else. The Opportunity Cost is the cost of the missed opportunity.

For example:

> Imagine you earn $70 an hour. Your house is dirty and needs a good clean. You have a choice: (A) you can clean the house yourself, or (B) you can engage a cleaner to clean your house.
>
> If you choose option (A) and it takes you three hours to clean your house, that clean just cost you:
>
> - $210 of your time (that's an expensive clean!); and
> - the Opportunity Cost of that clean includes the lost pleasure of doing something you enjoy doing, such as time with your kids or 3 hours of lost productive work time that might well have led to great opportunities (such as picking up a new client and lots of value).

If you choose option (B) and the cleaner charges you $22 an hour, and, being an expert he can clean your home in 2.5 hours rather than 3 hours, that clean just cost you $55, and:

- you have reclaimed 3 hours a week of your own lost time. Time you can spend with your family, growing your business, or on some *Me Time*
- at your hourly rate you have made $155 instead of $210 (because you had to pay the cleaner $55).

— *What other women say* —

Nicola Moras, Kickass Marketing Mentor

You need to ask yourself all of the time – what is the most valuable use of my time? And then focus on that.

Ruth MacKay, Managing Director, OURTEL Solutions

I have a cleaner come in once a week. I didn't used to take Opportunity Costs in to account with outsourcing at home ... but I am getting better at doing this as I get older. Too bad I did not do it when my daughter was younger so I could have had more quality time with her back then!

Anoushka Gungadin, CEO, The Duke of Edinburgh's International Award – Victoria

For me, Opportunity Cost both in financial and emotional terms completely justifies outsourcing as a perfect solution.

Oh, and by the way, here are the current commercial rates for some domestic helpers:

- A cleaner will cost you around $22 an hour
- A housekeeper will cost you around $25 an hour
- A gardener will cost you around $18 an hour
- A nanny will cost you around $22 an hour*

**all rates sourced from BaM www.babysittersandmore.com.au current at time of printing. Check the website for current rates.*

Emotional and Physical Costs - ouch, that hurts!

Not everyone identifies with the concept of Opportunity Cost. Or, while you might identify with the Opportunity Cost of some of your tasks, for other tasks the Emotional or Physical Costs will resonate far more strongly.

Looking back at the Opportunity Cost example above, I want to add another consideration, and that's the ROI on the investment you just made in engaging a cleaner. The house is sparkling, you don't have to clean the toilets yourself, you aren't tired and cranky and you are already feeling less stressed and less guilty because you just spent 3 hours of quality time with your kids.

The Emotional Cost of how you choose to spend your time can be a huge issue for women who try to juggle their career or business growth and their responsibilities as mums. There is a constant tension between our drive to succeed at work and our desire to be present with our children.

As already discussed, there will always be trade-offs when it comes to how you choose to manage your time. There will be times where you are needed at work but equally needed at home. What you choose to do in any given scenario will be informed by both rational decision making and by emotional decision making. And sometimes you will make the wrong choice. And when you do? Well, you know what happens - you are racked with guilt, you beat yourself up, you question your Values and priorities, and you self-talk up a virtual tornado of criticism and self-loathing.

With Physical Costs, this one isn't rocket science folks. Depending on the state of your physical health, there will be some tasks in your Standard Day that you simply should not do. I'm not a doctor, but in my learned opinion, if it hurts a lot then stop.

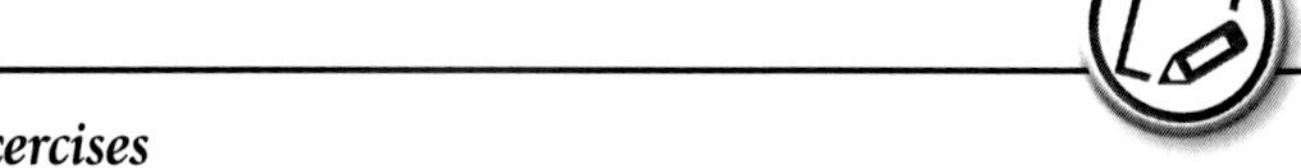

Exercises

Purpose

There are 3 exercises below which will help you identify your unique Emotional and Physical Costs.

Exercise 1 - My Emotional Costs

With Emotional Costs, your Values are very important. If you are not using your time in a way which is consistent with your Values, you will probably be feeling guilty, stressed and conflicted.

Actions:

- Grab your *Me Time* Workbook and flip back to your Top Values.
- Review your Standard Day Time Sheet and identify

any task/use of your time which brings with it an Emotional Cost. For example, if you have identified *Family-oriented* as your Number One Value and yet you work around the clock and put work before your family every day, you either need to be more honest with yourself about your actual priorities, or the current use of your time will be exacting an enormous Emotional Cost.

My Top Values:

Emotional Costs:

Alice's Me Time Diary

My Top Values:

~ *Successful*
~ *Family-oriented*
~ *Fit & Healthy*
~ *Loving*
~ *Integrity*
~ *Ethical*
~ *Financially secure*
~ *Adventurous*
~ *Respected*
~ *Independent*

Emotional Costs:

I am confident that I have identified my Values and that I have them in the right order, but as I look through my Standard Day it's pretty clear that I haven't been true to my actual priorities.

It's a bit confronting to reflect on how often I am yelling at or nagging the kids, rather than enjoying them. Just awesome to have 'Family-oriented' as my Number 2 priority, but to spend most of my family time screaming like a banshee. I also hadn't given it enough thought, but John and I have no real quality time together where we just enjoy each other's company without being exhausted. That's not great for our family or for our marriage. And time for myself? Well, I squeeze in a jog where I can, but that's hardly promoting my Number 3 priority of being 'Fit & Healthy'.

I am on the go the whole time, and it's just not sustainable. Something is going to have to give. I don't want to be an over-tired, over-worked, yelling, angry cow who hasn't the time or the energy to spend quality time with my kids, my husband or by myself. Shit it.

Exercise 2 - My Physical Costs

Actions:

- With Physical Costs, you need to listen to your body. If you are spending time during your Standard Day on tasks which cause you physical discomfort, or outright pain, then your use of time is exacting a Physical Cost that may no longer make sense to you. Examples include back pain, neck pain, headaches, chronic indigestion, nervous complaints, shoulder pain, wrist pain, knee pain, high blood pressure and so on.
- Similarly, if you have put on weight because you haven't had the time to exercise, or you have increased your visits to the doctor due to fatigue, these are Physical Costs you need to consider.
- In your *Me Time* Workbook, review your Standard Day Time Sheet and identify any task/use of your time which brings with it a Physical Cost.
- Depending on the severity of your Physical Costs, you should consider consulting a doctor.

My Physical Costs:

Alice's Me Time Diary

My Physical Costs:

Sitting all day at my desk is bad for my back and neck. I need to get up more often and stretch and walk.

More so, vacuuming the kitchen each day is just killing my back - I think that when I vacuum with one arm while leaning my weight on the nearest surface with my other arm, that's probably a good indication that vacuuming is exacting a Physical Cost. I even resort to sitting on the couch to vacuum under the coffee table to stave away the pain of bending.

I guess that falling asleep on the couch doesn't help the old back either.

I can't afford for my back to go again. Last time I was in bed unable to move for 4 days and I had to crawl to and from the toilet. When I was finally upright I looked like the Leaning Tower Of Pisa. I remember my Physio telling me that to get better I needed to 'get in touch with my pelvic floor'.

'Dear Pelvic Floor, It has been some time since we were last in touch. I recall vaguely having some contact with you before Henry was born, but gee, that would be a good 11 years ago! So, how the hell have you been?'

Yeah right. Ciao Ciao Pelvic Floor ... it was nice knowing you.

Exercise 3 - a Summary of my Costs

Actions:

- You have identified the Opportunity, Emotional and Physical Costs of how you use your time.
- Summarise these in the table below as this will allow you to sanity check your Musts, Wants, Delegates and Rejects.

	Summary of your personal costs
Opportunity Costs	
Emotional Costs	
Physical Costs	

Alice's Me Time Diary

	Summary of your personal costs
Opportunity Costs	*$70 an hour of my time plus the opportunities I forego - imagine if I used just 1 hour of that time to win a new client! There would be a bonus in that . . . hmmm.* *Frankly, doing some of these tasks at the rate of $70 an hour of my time is just ludicrous.*
Emotional Costs	*Yelling* *Feeling like a crap mum* *Feeling like a crap wife* *Grumpy* *Angry* *Guilty* *Stressed* *Over it* *Absolutely no libido whatsoever*
Physical Costs	*If my back goes again, I am screwed* *Tired, all the time*

How much did you say that was?

Now that you know what your personal time habits are costing, you need to stress test your Musts, Wants, Delegates and Rejects against:

- the Opportunity, Emotional and Physical Costs you have identified, and
- your Top Values.

This will give you a very different perspective of the value of your time, by testing whether the tasks you spend the majority of your time on are costing you at some level, and are inconsistent with your Values.

As a result, you may decide to move some of your Musts to Rejects or move some of your Musts to Delegates. That's OK - this is what this process is all about.

Exercises

Purpose

There are 3 exercises below. Their purpose is to stress test your Musts, Wants, Delegates and Rejects.

Exercise 1 - Stress testing my Time against the Costs

Actions:

- Grab your *Me Time* Workbook and your Standard Day Time Sheet/s.
- Revisit each task in Column 1 and consider whether continuing to do it will exact an Opportunity, Emotional or Physical Cost that you are no longer prepared to accept.
- Against each task, complete Column 4 using the following key:

- OK to continue the task = OK
- Opportunity Cost = OC
- Emotional Cost = EC
- Physical Cost = PC

- For any task you have previously identified as a Must or a Want, but which you now feel is costing you too much (at an Opportunity, Emotional or Physical level), consider very carefully the need to change those tasks to a Delegate or a Reject. Mark up any changes to Column 2.
- At this point in time, don't worry about *how* you are going to achieve the switch from doing a task to *not doing* a task - we will get to that soon. For now, you simply need to have a clear view of what you want to stop doing because the Opportunity, Emotional or Physical Costs simply no longer make sense.

◇◇

Alice's Me Time Diary

(Note: An extract of Alice's Standard Day is included below. For a full copy of Alice's Standard Day go to www.timestylers.com.au)

	Column 1	Column 2	Column 3	Column 4
Time spent	Weekday	Must/Want/ Delegate/Reject	$ Spend	Costs
5-6am	Sleep	Must		OK
6-7am	Get up 30 min jog ~~10~~ 5 min shower 5 min ~~including~~ wiping down shower 5 min make brekky for myself 5 mins Kids make own brekky ~~and kids~~ 5 min eat brekky 5 min stand in front of fridge and make mental shopping list	Must Want Must Delegate Must Delegate Must Reject	 $35 $6 $6 $6 $6 $6 $6	OK OK OK PC OK EC OK OC

7-8am	*10 min make kids lunches*	*Must*	*$12*	*OC*
	10 min tidy up after everyone's brekky	*~~Must~~Delegate*	*$12*	*EC*
	10 min find Henry's sports clothes	*~~Must~~Delegate*	*$12*	*EC*
	5 min nag kids to brush teeth	*Reject*	*$6*	*EC*
	15 min get dressed and throw on some makeup	*Must*	*$18*	*OK*
	5 min pack my bag	*Must*	*$6*	*OK*
	5 min yelling at kids to hurry up	*Reject*	*$6*	*EC*
8-9am	*10 min drive kids to school and do the drop and run*	*~~Must~~Delegate?*	*$12*	*OC*
	30 min drive into town, making work calls	*Must*	*$35*	*OK*
	5 min park car and walk to office building	*Must*	*$6*	*OK*
	10 min grab takeaway coffee	*Want*	*$12*	*OK*
	5 min hellos as I walk to my office	*Want*	*$6*	*OK*

noon-1pm	*15 min grab some sushi*	*Want*	*$18*	*OK*
	20 min at supermarket grabbing essentials for tonight	*~~Must~~ Reject*	*$23*	*OC*
	15 eating sushi while surfing internet	*Must*	*$18*	*OK*
	10 min make cup of coffee and chat	*~~Want~~ Reject*	*$12*	*OC*

5-6pm	*30 min drive to school to collect kids, making work calls*	*~~Must~~ Delegate*	*$35*	*OC*
	5 min drive kids to after-school activities, making work calls.	*~~Must~~ Delegate*	*$6*	*OC*
	Drop Olive at dance class (there is no way I am going to stay and watch!) and Henry at basketball			
	25 min dash home and clean kitchen, chuck some chemicals down the toilet and give a quick brush and flush, stand in front of fridge again thinking about what I need	*~~Must~~ Delegate*	*$29*	*PC/OC*
6-7pm	*5 min bring in washing and pour washing on to yesterday's pile of washing*	*~~Must~~ Delegate*	*$6*	*PC*
	20 min start dinner	*Must*	*$23*	*OK*
	5 min pick kids up from activities	*Must*	*$6*	*OK*
	5 min get kids set up with homework	*Must*	*$6*	*OK*
	15 min start folding washing, help with homework, turn on bath, put chickens away and collect eggs, feed cat	*Delegate*	*$18*	*PC/OC*
	10 keep an eye on dinner and tidy up kitchen, working like a maniac here	*Must*	*$12*	*OK*
7-8pm	*15 min get kids in bath, finish dinner prep, tidying as I go, set table*	*Must*	*$18*	*OK*
	20 min get kids out of bath, yell at them to stop fighting, yell at them to get into their PJs, yell at them to put their homework away, put their homework away myself, yell at them to get their lunch boxes out of their bags, get the lunch boxes out of their bags myself, yell at them to put their folded clothes away, do that myself too.	*Delegate*	*23*	*EC*
	25 min eat dinner	*Mus*	*$29*	*OK*

8-9pm	*20 min read with kids while John clearing table and loading dishwasher*	*Want*	*$23*	*OK*
	10 min cuddle kids and put them to bed, try not to fall asleep myself	*Want*	*$12*	*OK*
	20 min talk with John. Who? Oh yes, I remember you. My husband	*Want*	*$23*	*OK*
	10 min vacuum kitchen floor, finish the dishes, put leftovers away	~~*Must*~~ *Delegate*	*$12*	*PC*
9-10pm	*15 min tidy up all the kids' crap*	*Delegate*	*$18*	*PC/EC*
	20 min check Facebook	*Reject*	*$23*	*PC*
	10 min check diary for tomorrow	*Must*	*$12*	*OK*
	Fall asleep on couch	*Reject*		*PC*

Based on the Costs to me of using my time in this way, there are actually a LOT MORE tasks here that I can Delegate or Reject. Interesting. I need to sort this stuff out. Soon

Exercise 2 - Stress Test my Time against my Values

Actions:

- If you are not spending the majority of your time on what is most important to you, then you are either living under a lot of stress and guilt because your time spend does not reflect your Values, or you need to revisit your Values and priorities.
- In your *Me Time* Workbook, flip back to your Values which you placed in priority order.
- In Column 2, against each task you have identified as a Must and a Want - sanity check to see whether you are being true to your Values. Place a tick or a cross depending on your answer.
- Against each task you have identified as a Delegate or Reject - sanity check that you have not actually earmarked something you value as a task you are going

to get rid of. If you have, then either your Values need to be tweaked, or the task is actually a Want or a Must and you need to realign it. Place a tick or a cross, as appropriate.

Alice's Me Time Diary

My Values, in order of priority are:

1. *Successful*
2. *Family-oriented*
3. *Fit & Healthy*
4. *Loving*
5. *Integrity*
6. *Ethical*
7. *Financially secure*
8. *Adventurous*
9. *Respected*
10. *Independent*

I actually got most of this right when I cross checked it against my Values. But these are the areas I need to address:

	Column 1	Column 2	Column 3	Column 4
Time spent	Weekday	Must/Want/ Delegate/Reject	$ Spend	Costs
5-6am	*Sleep*	*Must* ✓		*OK*
6-7am	*Get up* *30 min jog* *~~10~~ 5 min shower* *5 min ~~including~~ wiping down shower* *5 min make brekky for myself* *5 mins Kids make own brekky ~~and kids~~* *5 min eat brekky* *5 min stand in front of fridge and make mental shopping list*	*Must* ✓ *Want* ✓ *Must* ✓ *Delegate* ✓ *Must* ✓ *Delegate* ✓ *Must* ✓ *Reject* ✓	 *$35* *$6* *$6* *$6* *$6* *$6* *$6*	*OK* *OK* *OK* *PC* *OC* *OC* *OK* *OC*

7-8am	10 min make kids lunches 10 min tidy up after everyone's brekky 10 min find Henry's sports clothes 5 min nag kids to brush teeth 15 min get dressed and throw on some makeup 5 min pack my bag 5 min yelling at kids to hurry up	Must ✓ ~~Must~~ Delegate ✓ ~~Must~~ Delegate ✓ Reject ✓ Must ✓ Must ✓ Reject ✓	$12 $12 $12 $6 $18 $6 $6	OC EC EC EC OK OK EC
8-9am	10 min drive kids to school and do the drop and run 30 min drive into town, making work calls 5 min park car and walk to office building 10 min grab takeaway coffee 5 min hellos as I walk to my office	Delegate? X Must ✓ Must ✓ Want ✓ Want ✓	$12 $23 $12 $23 $12	OC OK OK OK PC

noon-1pm	115 min grab some sushi 20 min at supermarket grabbing essentials for tonight 15 eating sushi while surfing internet 10 min make cup of coffee and chat	Want ✓ Reject ✓ Must ✓ ~~Want~~ Reject ✓	$18 $23 $18 $12	OK OC OK OC

5-6pm	30 min drive to school to collect kids, making work calls 5 min drive kids to after-school activities, making work calls. Drop Olive at dance class (there is no way I am going to stay and watch!) and Henry at basketball 25 min dash home and clean kitchen, chuck some chemicals down the toilet and give a quick brush and flush, stand in front of fridge again thinking about what I need	~~Must~~ Delegate ✓ ~~Must~~ Delegate ✓ ~~Must~~ Delegate ✓	$35 $6 $29	OC OC PC/OC
6-7pm	5 min bring in washing and pour washing on to yesterday's pile of washing 20 min start dinner 5 min pick kids up from activities 5 min get kids set up with homework 25 min start folding washing, help with homework, turn on bath, put chickens away and collect eggs, feed cat, start dinner, working like a maniac here	~~Must~~ Delegate ✓ Must X Must ✓ Must ✓ Delegate ✓	$6 $23 $6 $6 $18 $12	PC OK OK OK PC/OC OK
7-8pm	15 min get kids in bath, finish dinner prep, tidying as I go, set table 30 min get kids out of bath, yell at them to stop fighting, yell at them to get into their PJs, yell at them to put their homework away, put their homework away myself, yell at them to get their lunch boxes out of their bags, get the lunch boxes out of their bags myself, yell at them to put their folded clothes away, do that myself too. 15 min eat dinner	Must ✓ Delegate ✓ Must ✓	$18 $23 $29	OK EC OK

Continued …

... continued

8-9pm	20 min read with kids while John clearing table and loading dishwasher 10 min cuddle kids and put them to bed, try not to fall asleep myself 20 min talk with John. Who? Oh yes, I remember you. My husband 10 min vacuum kitchen floor, finish the dishes, put leftovers away	Want X Want ✓ Want ✓ ~~Must~~ Delegate ✓	$23 $12 $23 $12	OK OK OK PC
9-10pm	15 min tidy up all the kids' crap 20 min check Facebook 10 min check diary for tomorrow Fall asleep on couch	Delegate ✓ Reject ✓ Must ✓ Reject ✓	$18 $23 $12	PC/EC PC OK PC

- *Making the kids lunches - I actually enjoy this (strange I know), and it also means I know that they are getting a healthy, nutritional lunch. If I left it up to them to make their own lunch, God knows what they would choose to eat. But, I do plan to educate them on this better - I will get them to make their lunches with me, that way they can learn what is good to eat and I can also transition them to making their own lunch.*
- *Driving the kids to school - the days they don't want to ride their bikes, I will take them. I like to have a chat with them in the morning.*
- *Setting the kids up for homework - I can do this a bit smarter. Like making the lunches, I will work alongside the kids so they can learn how to set themselves up properly, and then I will help them with anything they don't understand.*
- *If I delegate school pick-up, then I won't have to rush home in such a frenzy. Plus, whoever I delegate this to can start the meal prep for me. Hey, this is a smart idea!*
- *It also makes sense to delegate the clearing of the table to the kids - if we split this up then both John and I can put the kids to bed together.*

Damn it, I still feel guilty about not watching Olive at dance class. She keeps asking me to stay and watch 'like the other mums'. And I know some mums can think of nothing more joyous than watching their child hop around in a pink tutu, but not me. But, if I don't do it I'II continue to be racked with guilt. I hate mother guilt! I know Family-oriented is my second priority, but too bad. I just can't do dance. I will do something else with her.

How do you feel?

Analysing where you spend your time, and what that is costing you, can be challenging. This is completely understandable - you are breaking down your time and analysing it to within an inch of its life. It's bound to be confronting!

Exercise 3 - Time for Reflection

Action:

Write down a few thoughts about how you feel right now:

I feel:

Alice's Me Time Diary

I feel:

My God. I can't believe this. I knew that I was carrying the bulk of chores around the house, and that it probably wasn't the best use of my time, but costing it out financially finally proves to me that I have been living like a lunatic. And I thought I was managing my time quite well. I was deluded.

I haven't even started on my weekends yet.

My hourly rate is $70. It took me four hours to clean the house on Sunday - damn, that clean just cost me $280! Plus if I factor in that I was cleaning on my day off, eating into family time, and on a Sunday (penalty rates surely?), the Opportunity Cost is ridiculous. I could have had an expert clean my house - and even if it took them 4 hours, which I doubt - for $88! Even when I include the costs of the cleaner, I would still be well ahead at my hourly rate. And then I think about what I could have been doing with those four hours - a family adventure (living my Values, right!?), reading a book and relaxing, going for a bike ride with the kids.

Speaking of kids - tidying up after the kids for 3 hours a week is costing me $210!

Going to the supermarket 4 or 5 times a week is costing me a fortune in time!

John is going to have a heart attack when I tell him that his efforts at mowing the lawn (pretty badly if the truth be known), cost us $100. Ha!

Shit. It's not funny.

Are you serious?

Before we finish Step 3 Analyse, don't you want to know how many hours you have now identified as hours you can potentially reclaim?

Exercise - Add up your Time Savings

Purpose

Having undertaken the second cut of your time in a Standard Day, it's rewarding to calculate how many hours you can save if you implement all of your Delegates and Rejects. This is the best bit!

		Total
A	The number of hours I will save each day if I delegate everything in my Delegate list	
B	The number of hours I will save each day if I discard or better manage everything in my Rejects list	
C	(A + B) x 30 days = the number of hours I can get back each Month	

Alice's Me Time Diary

		Total
A	The number of hours I will save each day if I delegate everything in my Delegate list	*3 hours*
B	The number of hours I will save each day if I discard or better manage everything in my Rejects list	*1 hour*
C	(A + B) x 30 days = the number of hours I can get back each Month *180 min + 60 min = 240 x 30 days = 7200 mins = 120 hours*	*120 hours*

Holy shit! Are you kidding me?

Nice Work. Now You Know:

- The Tasks you perform in a Standard Day (Column 1)
- Your Musts, Wants, Delegates and Rejects (Column 2)
- The financial cost of your time spend based on your hourly rate (Column 3)
- The Opportunity, Emotional and Physical Costs of how you spend your time
- You have stress tested your Musts, Wants, Delegates and Rejects against the Opportunity, Emotional and Physical Costs
- You have aligned your time spend back to your Values
- There is a whole lot of time sitting there waiting for you to get it back - are you ready to go get it?

It's time to REFRAME.

STEP 4: REFRAME

Trust the process

The potential number of hours you can reclaim which you identified at the end of Step 3 Analyse may, just like Alice's, seem to you to be a little, well, unreal. However, don't forget that those savings reflect what is up for grabs if you choose to Delegate and Reject every single thing you have identified as a Delegate or Reject. You may not choose to do so. All we are aiming for at this point in time is finding you 30 hours a month.

You need to trust the process.

With a clear idea of your Musts, Wants, Delegates and Rejects, along with the Opportunity, Emotional and Physical Costs of your current time management habits, it's now time to Reframe.

Step 4 Reframe will give you the theory, along with 5 Exercises and 7 Actions you need to complete to convert the theory into reality (the 7 Actions are picked up by Alice in her Action Plan in Step 5 Take Control). This is where all of the work you have done so far comes together and you start to get back hours of quality time a month.

How exciting!

This will take work. No-one ever said that changing a habit or establishing a new habit was going to be easy. If it was, you wouldn't need any help at all. However, if you do the work, you will get back 30 hours of time to live the life you want. Now that has got to be worth it. Yes?

◇◇

Alice's Me Time Diary

If this is true, if I can really get back more than 120 hours a month, then I am in. You had me at It's Time.

I am now on a mission. A Time Transformation mission!

This is where the rubber hits the road.

I am no longer prepared to live like a lunatic.

Hasta la vista housework!

I love a good idiom, not to mention a healthy synonym and a good movie quote.

All good. Time to Reframe. Stop procrastinating Alice, that was the old you.

◇◇

Managing your time the SMART way

Musts - a whole world of awesomeness

Your Musts are the essential things you need to do. The vast majority of your time will be Musts - for example, unless you are an heiress you will need to earn money, which means you will need to keep working. Working for a living is a Must for most of us.

Having said that, you also want to be in a position where the vast majority of the tasks you have identified as Musts are things you actually enjoy doing, the awesome stuff. If not, then much of the time you spend will be pretty miserable with you plodding along doing a mountain of tasks that you have little interest in or passion for.

Run your eye over your Musts because you want to get this as right as possible:

- For those Musts that you don't enjoy but which are temporary (such as watching ballet practice) you either need to suck it up (this time will pass, trust me) or Delegate or Reject it. Simple.
- For those Musts that you don't enjoy doing all the time but which you don't mind doing some of the time (such as vacuuming) consider changing it to a Delegate and then vacuum once a week to keep things under control. Simple.
- For those Musts which you don't enjoy at all and which take up much of your time (such as work days full of meetings) think about how you can reframe your day to reduce the number of meetings, or at least delegate to your team. Harder. But at least you now know this is an area you need to work on.

Don't worry if you aren't 100% sure that you have your Musts settled. This is an iterative process and you will continue to refine your Musts, Wants, Delegates and Rejects during the 5 *Steps to Being SMART*, and then again over time as your life or circumstances change.

If you are satisfied that you mostly have your Musts nailed, the SMART way to manage your Musts is to schedule time in for them. This will be covered in Step 5 Take Control and in Part 3, *Me Time* Top Tools.

In the meantime, let's make this real!

Alice's Me Time Diary

After doing a few cuts in Step 3 Analyse and a deep dive of my Standard Day, my Costs and double checking my Values, I'm pretty happy that I mostly have the Musts right.

Delegate - or detonate

Delegate is the Time Segment I am most passionate about! This is the stuff that definitely floats my boat. The reason why you delegate the things you don't want to do, is to give yourself time for the things you do want to do. It's not rocket science.

You probably delegate at work, so, why not at home? Because, be rest assured, there are plenty of tasks you are probably doing on the home front that you could (and should) Delegate. So, let's Delegate.

Delegates are broken into two groups -

Insource: These are the tasks you don't want to pay someone to do. This includes everything you currently do at home for the people you live with (partner and/or kids) that they need to start doing for themselves. Funnily enough, what you may have lost sight of is that you are a mum and/or partner, not a slave.

Outsource: These are the tasks that you are prepared to pay someone to do. Remember that when you Outsource, you are getting an expert who will in all likelihood do a much better and quicker job that you. Also from an Opportunity, Emotional or Physical Cost perspective you now know that it makes sense to pay someone else to do this stuff.

Insourcing

Family is a team sport.

The best way to Insource is to make each person in your home accountable for their own stuff - they are capable of tidying away their own belongings, hanging up their own towels, making their own beds, putting away their own clothes and so on. Happily, the list of what your family can do for themselves is endless.

There will also be a stack of general chores that can be done by anyone in your home, which can be divided between your family members. Some of these are even fun, that your kids will fight for (like making and lighting the fire, which also means cleaning up last night's fire).

— *What other women say* —

Tanya McVicar, Head of Operational Risk & Compliance, Personal Banking at National Australia Bank

My kids get pocket money for doing the general family chores, such as taking out the bins. They don't get paid for tidying up their own crap. It's their crap after all.

Carolyn Creswell, Founder Carman's

When I ask my kids to do something I always give them a choice. Do you want to take the rubbish out? I might get a response of 'Why me?' My response is 'Who do you think should do it? I am cooking, but if you want to cook I will do the rubbish'. You just have to keep on them- we are a family.

Now that you are clever and smart it's time to BE STRONG.

Remember *Your Commitment?* It will come in handy here. Right about now the thought of the fights you will have in getting your kids, and maybe even your partner, to actually manage their own crap might get that little voice in your head chattering away. Let's knock that on the head right now.

The 3 traps not to fall into:

1. ***OMG, the kids (not to mention my partner) have left their wet towels on the floor again! How many times do I have to ask them to hang their towels up? Honestly, I am not their [insert swear word of choice] slave!***

And then what do you do? Well, you pick the wet towels up off the floor and re-hang them.

You know you do this. Is it any wonder that your family don't pick up their towels for themselves? If you were living in a hotel where the towels you left on the bathroom floor were (miraculously it seems) collected, washed, refreshed and re-hung every single day, you would probably leave your towel on the floor too. Be honest.

I am not blaming you. I am just telling you that you are a major part of the problem.

Actions:

- You need to break two habits here - the habit of your family who are used to leaving their crap lying around because they know you will pick it up and put it away, and your habit of picking it up and putting it away.
- Get them to pick up their own towels, and if they don't? Well, no-one likes to dry themselves with a wet smelly towel - they will get the message eventually.

2. ***I just can't be bothered nagging my kids (not to mention my partner) every single day to get them to help me. I sound like a harpy. It's just easier for me to do it myself.***

That's true. You do sound like a harpy. And yes it would be easier to do it yourself. But both of these small facts don't change the bigger fact that if you want to reclaim back lost time, you need to stop doing the basics for your family.

Your children and partner are entirely capable of doing this stuff for themselves. You are establishing new habits for them as well as for you.

Actions:

- This will take 30 days. If necessary be a harpy for 30 days.
- You are not doing your family any favours by doing this stuff for them. It's never too early for your kids, and it's never too late for your partner, to learn some self-sufficiency. So if you can't let go of being their slave for yourself, just kid yourself that you are doing it for them.
- Again, your family will eventually get the message. And when they do, make sure you tell them how awesome they are (even if it did take them 8.5 and 45 years respectively before they learnt to hang up their own towel for the first time ...).

— *What other women say* —

Renee Ackary, co-owner of Cocohoney Salon, Seddon

One salon I worked for hired a 17-year-old girl to help out with the basics - sweeping up the hair, folding the towels, mopping the floor. I actually had to show her how to use a broom. When it came to mopping, she didn't know that she had to wring the mop out after dipping it in the bucket!

There was water everywhere. When I asked her what happened she confessed that she had never used a mop, broom or a vacuum. Her mum did everything at her house. Where were her life skills?

Holly Kramer, CEO Best & Less

I definitely Insource. Kids have to have chores - they need it for discipline.

Carolyn Creswell, Founder Carman's

I delegate to my mum and I give her specific tasks to do. I utilise the people in my life who are happy to help out.

Janine Allis, Founder and Managing Director
Boost Juice (Retail Zoo)

My husband is really good - he does equally as much housework. I have a great Personal Assistant who manages both work and personal stuff for me. And my mum is an enormous help.

Fatima Dib, Business Owner, Smart Financial Solutions

My aunt had a very aggressive cancer. She told me that she needed to survive for another 5 months so that she could teach her children everything they needed to know about living independently and self-sufficiently. That was so confronting for me. I went home and that very night I started teaching my daughters how to make a basic dinner. I haven't stopped since. It's so important to give our children the skills they need to survive without us.

3. It's not that hard for me to do the small stuff. Really. It only takes me 5 minutes.

No, it does not. It's time for a reality check – the small stuff which you think only takes 5 minutes actually eats up hours and hours of your life. If you don't believe this, I urge you to conduct your own experiment on the small stuff you do.

Actions:

- Keep a diary for a couple of days and jot down all the crazy, time sucking, small stuff chores you do which you could insource. Note how long they take you to do, and then do the maths. You will be horrified.
- There is a template for adding up your Small Stuff in the *Me Time* Workbook. Use it.

◇◇

Alice's Me Time Diary

I love a challenge.

For the purposes of my own scientific research I timed the small stuff and clearly they just ain't so small after all. The small stuff certainly does not take '5 minutes'. Here are the results of my own research, rounded to the nearest hour (*note, not performed under internationally recognised scientific conditions such as having a control group and such other technical requirements which I don't actually recall from secondary school science class. Rather, just performed by me in my own home with my stopwatch).*

The Small Stuff I do around the house which I thought took 5 minutes and how long it REALLY takes:

	Daily tally	Annual tally in hours (x 365 days)	Annual total in days (a day being 12 hours)
Pick up wet towels and re-hang	*1 min*	*6 hours*	*½ a day per year!*
Make the kid's beds	*3 mins*	*18 hours*	*1½ days of my life per year*

Find the dirty washing on the floor, under the bed, and in the sports bags and put it in the wash	*6 mins*	*36 hours*	*3 days of my life per year*
Tidying away the iPods, iPads, homework, books, shoes, basketballs, work and other kid/husband paraphernalia left out from the night before	*12 mins*	*73 hours*	*6 days of my life per year*
Clearing the table, putting the salt and pepper away, scraping the plates, rinsing the plates, stacking the dishwasher and wiping the table	*7 mins*	*43 hours*	*3½ days of my life per year*
Folding and putting away the kids'/husband's clean clothes, clean linen and towels	*6 mins*	*36 hours*	*3 days of my life per year*
Total per annum		*212 hours*	*18 days of my life each year!*

Holy Shit. John! JOHN! Come here and check this out!

◇◇

So, there you go. Hell, if you want to spend 18 days a year cleaning up after your family when they have the skill set to do it themselves, please, knock yourself out.

For mine, I recommend you be a harpy for 30 days. You get the picture. BE STRONG.

> Oh, and by the way, if you currently do all of the above *small stuff* chores every day and you STOP for just one month, you just gained back 18 hours for that month. That's over halfway towards your 30 hours. Yep. Think about that!

I trust you are ready to Insource?

Exercise - It's all about Insourcing

Purpose

To work out what your family can do for themselves so that you get back hours of lost time.

Actions:

- Get out the Insourcing template.
- Identify everything that you think can be insourced in your house and write up your Insourcing List.
- Make sure your Insourcing List is tailored to your family and your needs, for example, if you don't have a dishwasher, the dishes can be done by hand, dried and then put away (potentially a job for one or three separate jobs).
- Sit down with your kids and partner to brainstorm what else can be added. Getting the family involved in this way will help with their buy in. Explain why, as a family, you now insource. Get everyone to agree that *Family is a Team Sport*. Make sure everyone is clear on what they are responsible for.
- Make multiple copies of your Insourcing List and stick it on the fridge and in other obvious places (like your kids' bedroom walls). Or copy the Insourcing List on to a whiteboard and keep it in the kitchen.
- From now on, when you see your family's stuff lying around just begging you to pick it up, clear it away, tidy it or make it magically disappear, take a deep breath, back out of the room and quietly shut the door.
- Be a harpy. Remind your family of what they agreed to do. As much as your harpy voice annoys you it will annoy them more.

- You might also decide to assign a cash reward (pocket money) to the big ticket items.

Here is an extract of the Insourcing List, start jotting down your ideas here:

Insourcing List	
Daily Tasks	Who
Rotating weekly tasks (include frequency)	Who
Up for grabs and cash	

Alice's Me Time Diary

I am LOVING this! There are so many jobs I can insource to my darling little loved ones that I wish I had more kids just so I had more people to insource to!

I have decided not to offer any financial incentive for these chores (apart from washing the cars). The fact is, my kids are not paying to stay at this hotel in which they reside, nor are they paying for the petrol for mum's taxi, or the school/dentist/never ending after-school activity fees, cash for footy cards, cash for movies, cash for hot chips after footy, cash for the sake of asking for cash. And so I am happy to let them work off some of their debt. Ha!

Besides which, family is a team sport. It's all about chipping in. It's all about having a good work ethic. Life wasn't meant to be easy. You weren't born with a silver spoon in your mouth.

(I have hundreds of these pointless little expressions which I am happy to throw out at will as required. However, sometimes it's quite alarming when I open my mouth and my mother comes out. This isn't over. I am going to keep adding and adding and adding to my lovely new Insourcing List.)

Insourcing List COMPLY OR DIE MY DARLINGS!	
Daily Tasks	**Who**
Tidy away your own stuff - laptops, phones, toys, school books, etc. Just because I have not included an item does not mean you don't have to tidy it up. Rule of thumb - if it belongs to you and you got it out, put it away.	*Henry and Olive*
Tidy your bedroom	*Henry and Olive*
Make your bed	*Henry and Olive*
Hang up your towel and spread it out so that it dries properly and doesn't smell gross	*Henry and Olive*
Fold your freshly cleaned clothes and put them away nicely	*Henry and Olive*
Unpack your lunchbox every day and check the bottom of your school bag for fruit and school notices	*Henry and Olive*
Vacuum your room (Saturday only)	*Henry and Olive*
Sort out your 'floordrobe'. Dirty clothes go in the wash and clean clothes go in the wardrobe. Funny that. Don't complain to me if don't have clean clothes.	*Henry and Olive*
Tidy away your own stuff	*John*
Pick your clothes up from the bedroom floor and put them away or in the wash. Don't complain to me if don't have clean clothes.	*John*
Hang up your towel	*John*
Put the toilet lid down, wipe your whiskers off the sink, put your toothbrush away, replace the toilet roll when it is finished, flush the toilet (twice if necessary).	*John*

Rotating weekly tasks (include frequency)	Who
Vacuum family areas : twice a week	*Weeks 1 & 3: Henry* *Weeks 2 & 4: Olive*
Stack and unstack dishwasher: daily	*Weeks 1 & 3: Olive* *Week 2 & 4: Henry*
Put the rubbish out: daily *Put the bins out and bring them in: weekly*	*Weeks 1 & 3: Henry* *Week 2 & 4: Olive*
Feed the pets: daily *Clean out the pet enclosures: weekly*	*Weeks 1 & 3: Olive* *Week 2 & 4: Henry*
Walk the dog/family time	*Family*
Up for grabs and cash	
Wash the cars $10	

— What other women say —

Carolyn Creswell, Founder Carman's

Put a sign on your fridge - 'Don't do anything for your kids that they are capable of doing for themselves". Kids need to help out, it's good for them.

Sarah Wood, Associate Director Workforce Strategy & Communications, People and Culture, Victoria University

I announced to my kids (aged 14 and 12) that they are now responsible for making their own lunch each morning. I gritted my teeth and prepared myself for an argument, however they accepted my decision without question. No longer making the school lunches has completely changed my mornings!

Outsourcing

Outsourcing is a simple, effective and efficient way to gain back significant hours of time.

Exercise - It's all about Outsourcing

Purpose

To work out the tasks you can pay someone else to do for you around your home.

Review the table below and put a tick next to each item that you know you would derive a benefit from outsourcing.

Actions:

- When you think about Outsourcing, revisit the tasks you have identified as Delegates in your Standard Day which you would quite happily pay for - keep in mind your Opportunity, Emotional and Physical Costs.
- The *Me Time* Workbook has an Outsourcing List which you can print out and then tick everything you want to outsource around your home.
- Complete your Outsourcing List and stick it on the fridge and next to your computer.
- From the items you have identified, choose one task to outsource from the first Monday of next month. Source your service providers via www.babysittersandmore.com.au, the Yellow Pages, online or via your friends - whatever works best for you.
- Choose a second item to implement from the first Monday of the second month.

- Choose a third item to implement from the first Monday of the third month.
- And so on.

— *What other women say* —

Anoushka Gungadin, CEO, The Duke of Edinburgh's International Award - Victoria

I outsource most maintenance related tasks in my house - cleaning, ironing, some baby-sitting and the garden. I believe there are experts in every field of life who are passionate about what they do. I leave the housekeeping to someone else. Then, the time I get back can either be spent doing fun things with my kids, outdoor and indoor activities, and helping them with homework.

I also think that I am able to support another person and his/her family.

Nicola Moras, Kickass Marketing Mentor

When it comes to outsourcing for the first time, my best advice is to look at everything you do and identify the things that you can outsource. Work out what it would cost you to do the job versus what it will cost to outsource.

I should have outsourced much sooner than I did!

Tanya McVicar, Head of Operational Risk & Compliance, Personal Banking at National Australia Bank

You may be a super cleaner, but if you can make more money working on your business or in your career than it costs to engage a cleaner then it's a no-brainer - you should outsource the cleaning.

Janine Allis, Founder and Managing Director Boost Juice (Retail Zoo)

I have a great cleaner with an attitude - she tells the kids off for their mess!

Holly Kramer, CEO Best & Less

I had no choice but to Outsource. My husband and I were both working full time in very demanding jobs and we needed help running the house.

Carolyn Creswell, Founder Carman's

I Outsource lots of tasks. I often Outsource when we are on holidays - I find a local, loving grandma to help us out.

Outsourcing List	Tick	Priority
Housekeeping		
Cleaning		
Meal planning and cooking		
Ironing		
Shopping		
De-cluttering		
Home management, paying bills, personal diary management		
Running errands; buy and wrap gifts		
House sitting		
Childcare - nanny		

Childcare - babysitting		
Mother's Helper		
Before/After-school care		
Tutoring		
Care/companionship for a parent		
Care/companionship for an infirm sibling or infirm adult child		
Pet sitting		
Dog walking		
Pet grooming		
Gardening and lawn mowing		
Landscaping		
Packing and moving		
Home maintenance		
Cleaning out the gutters		
Washing the windows		
Someone to put the new furniture together; set up the new TV; connect the WiFi		
Someone to wait for the plumber; the TV technician and so on		

Multi-taskers

Many of the service providers you want to engage are actually experts at more than one task. In addition, many will be looking for as much work as possible. So, it makes sense to group your tasks and find someone who will do them all. The benefits of this approach include:

- You only have to find, interview, trial and engage one person instead of two or more
- You only have to introduce one new person to the family
- You only have to show one person the way you want things done
- You only have to pay one person
- You will end up paying less because the service provider you engage can multi-task and will get your multiple tasks done more efficiently
- You will be offering more work to one person = win : win

For example:

You are looking for a ...	Be smart and find someone who will ...	Av cost per hour*
Cleaner	Clean Iron Periodically clean out the big ticket items (fridge and pantry) BYO equipment**	$22

Housekeeper	As above, plus: Tidy Supermarket shop Prepare meals for family Manage laundry, change linen, put all clothes away	$25
Nanny	Care for/entertain the kids Take to activities Tidy kids' areas Light cleaning Manage the kids' laundry Prepare food for the kids and basic prep for you Grab the essentials from the supermarket	$22
Mother's Helper	As above - plus: Full clean Supermarket shop Prepare meals for family Run errands	$25
Gardener	Do odd jobs Mow Weed Sweep Install a watering system BYO equipment**	$18

**sourced through www.babysittersandmore.com.au*

***Bonus! You don't have to buy or maintain the equipment!*

Alice's Me Time Diary

Outsourcing List	Tick	Priority
Housekeeping	✓	#1
Cleaning	✓	
Meal planning and cooking		
Ironing	✓	
Shopping		
De-cluttering	✓	
Home management, paying bills, personal diary management		
Running errands; buy and wrap gifts	✓	
House sitting		
Childcare - nanny		
Childcare - babysitting	✓	#4
Mother's Helper	✓	#2
Before/After-school care	✓	
Tutoring		
Care/companionship for a parent		
Care/companionship for an infirm sibling or infirm adult child		
Pet sitting	✓	

Dog walking		
Pet grooming		
Gardening and lawn mowing	✓	#3
Landscaping	✓	
Packing and moving		
Home maintenance		
Cleaning out the gutters	✓	
Washing the windows	✓	
Someone to put the new furniture together; set up the new TV; connect the WiFi	✓	
Someone to wait for the plumber; the TV technician and so on		

I was loving this, but now it's actually time to take action and make it real; I am starting to feel guilty again. Maybe I should just do this stuff myself?

NO WAY! I'm now clever and SMART. It's time to prove my smarts. I know this is the right thing to do, because:

~ *I am tired, angry and nasty, and I just can't go on like this. I want to be a happy, engaged and energetic mum.*

~ *The costs of doing this stuff myself don't make sense - I have done the maths.*

~ *I can get someone else to do this stuff for a lot less money than it will cost me at my own hourly rate.*

~ *I can use the time I save to spend time with my family, spend time on my own or spend time on my other Wants.*

~ *I am not an expert at these tasks. Most weeks I barely get to clean the toilets. The person I get to do these tasks will be an expert. I will end up with a better result in a faster time that it would have taken me. Plus, the kids won't catch a disease from the toilets.*

~ *Doing this stuff is definitely not the best use of my time.*

~ *I am not going to let anyone judge me for the decisions I make to Outsource - I certainly wasn't worried about being judged for not cleaning the toilets, so let's get a bit of perspective.*

OK. Feeling better again. I might write that list out in case I get chastised by John's Mum.

After costing my time it definitely makes sense to get a cleaner for 3 hours a week. It also makes a lot of sense in terms of not hurting my back in again. I thought John would vote this one down, but when he saw the Opportunity Cost analysis, plus when we thought about the costs of hiring in additional help if I did my back and was not able to do anything around the house, he was sold (but he only wants the cleaner once a fortnight at this stage - I will need to work on him).

We have agreed that we really are in desperate need to reconnect and to spend some time together without the kids. We are going to have a weekly date night. Need to arrange a babysitter. Kids feeling affronted that we want to go out together, without them. Too bad. Can't wait!

◇◇◇

Rejects - it won't hurt for long

I love the Rejects Time Segment almost as much as the Delegates Time Segment. This is where you can potentially pick up enormous amounts of time to add to your 30 hours a month. Your Rejects will fall into two camps:

Complete Rejects: The stuff that absolutely no-one needs to do, including you.

Partial Rejects: The stuff that needs to be done, but which can be done more efficiently.

— *What other women say* —

Holly Kramer, CEO Best & Less

Early on I Rejected the idea of cooking every night. We get take away twice a week. I also Reject ironing! I make sure I buy clothes that don't wrinkle.

Carolyn Creswell, Founder Carman's

Ebay is my friend. If the kids need school socks I just jump online and buy them. I don't hit the shops.

Janine Allis, Founder and Managing Director Boost Juice (Retail Zoo)

I don't go to any school things. I don't feel the need to go to the school Mother's Day stall. I remember once going to a school sports day and a mum came up and said to me 'Are you new?!' My son had been at the school for 6 years!

Natalie Gruzlewski, TV presenter and Aussie Farmers Direct ambassador

Since discovering Aussie Farmers Direct, spending less time in the supermarket has been a no brainer for me. As a busy mum, grocery shopping online is a huge time saver – that's an extra 2 hours a week just for me! I shop online when and where I like, using the Aussie Farmers 'Aisle One' app - which lets me stroll through a virtual supermarket, select all the nutritious produce my family needs and drag and drop it into my shopping basket. The best bit? It's delivered direct to my door and I don't have to be home when they drop it off. Brilliant! The time saving and convenience is key, but since Aussie Farmers Direct only deliver top quality, all-Australian produce, I also have the confidence of knowing where my food is really from - and that just by doing my shopping I'm supporting the great work of our Aussie farmers and producers.

Exercise - It's all about the Rejects

Purpose

To get time back by identifying what you can completely delete from your day.

Actions:

- Choose one task to Reject from the start of next month.
- Choose a second item to Reject from the start of the second month.
- Choose a third item to Reject from the start of the third month.
- And so on, until all of your Rejects are gone.
- Revisit your Standard Day from time to time - there will be more stupid habits you can Reject. Trust me.
- If something is a Complete Reject then don't let it sneak back into your day. You are getting rid of this for a reason. The reason is that it is a stupid use of your time.

You are getting good at these lists by now, and an extract of the Rejects List is below:

Complete Rejects - the stuff NO-ONE needs to do. Ever.	Priority

Partial Rejects - the stuff I can do smarter	

◇◇

Alice's Me Time Diary

Complete Rejects - the stuff NO-ONE needs to do. Ever.	Priority
Procrastinating over my Reject List!(Snort!)	
Putting myself last every single time (from now on there will be 'Me Time').	*#5*
Piling instead of filing and then shifting my piles from one room to another.	*#2*
Going to the supermarket at lunchtime or peak hour and then queueing for a car park, fighting for a trolley, queueing at the register, and queueing to get out of the carpark. *In fact - I am going to Reject supermarkets all together! It's time to shop online.*	*#1*
Running errands after school drop-off/pick-up when every man and his dog is also running errands.	*#3*
Procrastinating every morning about the first thing I need to do.	*#1*
Washing the dishes and then putting them through the dishwasher.	*#1*
Partial Rejects - the stuff I can do smarter	
Don't wait until things are out of control to do a massive clean-up. Get into the habit of putting things away as soon as I have finished with them.	*#4*
Don't go to the supermarket every day - shop online! *Make a weekly meal plan and have a good idea what I want to put in the lunch boxes. Work out what I need for the week and write a list.* *Once a month, shop at a large wholesaler and stock up on the non-perishables, so we always have the basics on hand.*	*#1*

Don't cook dinner every night; *(i) make extra because some meals just taste better the next day (like spaghetti bolognaise), and* *(ii) it's easy to cook a double batch and freeze half for another night, and* *(iii) John can cook too.* *If we do this often enough we will have a ready supply of nutritious meals on hand.*	*#1*
Don't get distracted by Facebook or Instagram or Pinterest or other social media! *I am going to keep Facebook closed so I'm not tempted to pop in when I hear an alert.* *Don't update my Facebook status every time I move. No-one cares if I am eating dinner except me. Really.*	*#1*
Stop with the constant checking of emails! *I am going to schedule 3-4 regular email checking time slots each day. Plus I am going to turn off my email alert.* *And no more checking my junk mail box just in case. It's junk for a reason.*	*#1*

Some of these are just so easy to change that I am going to make a number of them my number #1 priority and make the changes straight away. Nothing's going to stop me!

I am going to come back to this Reject List once I have all my Rejects under control because I definitely think there is more to be had.

The decision to shop online will be a game changer. I am going to try the Aussie Farmers Direct 'Aisle One' app! But it also means we will have to be more organised about planning the meals. That's OK, practise will make perfect.

Actually, there's a thought: I might workshop this one with the girls. There are bound to be plenty of other stupid time-wasting things I haven't thought of - I can put it out there for a bit of crowd sourcing on Facebook (hmmm, at a scheduled Facebook session such as morning tea time!) Definitely not just a random jump into Facebook, because I DON'T DO THAT ANYMORE (see Priority #1).

Oh dear, just realised I prioritised to stop 'Putting Myself Last every single time' as my last priority! Now that's irony for you. Clearly I am a work in progress.

◇◇

Wants - I want it, I want it, I want it!

Finally, you've made it! This is where you get to do all the awesome things you Want to do with your extra 30 hours. Your Wants are otherwise known as *Me Time,* just in case that's a concept you have never given consideration to.

Exercise - It's all about your Wants

Purpose

To start spending time on the things you really Want to spend time on.

Actions:

- You started filling out your Wants List in Step 1 Self Aware.
- The great thing about working through the *5 Steps to Being SMART* is that other possibilities might have opened up to you - new ideas now that you (and your partner) have extra time. Update your Wants List and keep it with you so you can add to it every time a new idea strikes you.
- From the items you have listed, start prioritising them and choose one task to enjoy from the start of next month.
- Choose a second item to enjoy from the start of the second month.
- Choose a third item to enjoy from the start of the third month, and so on.
- Give yourself permission to do and enjoy your Wants.
- And as you start to make more time, continue to add to and enjoy your Wants.
- The best way to manage your Wants is to schedule time for them - more on this in Step 5 Take Control and later in Part 3, *Me Time* Top Tools.
- Stay committed - don't let the Musts, Delegates or Rejects encroach on your *Me Time.*
- Chop, chop. Off you go. It's YOUR turn now.

— *What other women say* —

Megan Dalla-Camina, Strategist and Author

If I can give you one piece of advice, it is to get clear on what you want and then give yourself permission to have it. The permission piece is huge. It's hard to do. But once you have truly given yourself permission, the rest is just detail.

Ruth MacKay, Managing Director, OURTEL Solutions

The one thing I do for myself, my Me Time, is have a pedicure and/or a massage. Both make me feel so invigorated!

Holly Kramer, CEO Best & Less

When you do get back time, definitely your husband seems to come last! I decided to buy a Season pass to the theatre and that's become my night out with my husband. We meet in town and have a drink, watch a Play and then have dinner. Just make it happen - it's really nice.

My Wants List What I will do with my extra 30 hours a month	Priority

Alice's Me Time Diary

My Wants List What I will do with my extra 30 hours a month	Priority
Take up boxing	
Learn meditation	*#1*
Do a barista course	
Teach the kids to cook without yelling	
Hit the shops with a vengeance	
Jog more regularly	
Plan a family holiday - an adventure involving crocodiles	
PLUS:	
Date night once a week	*#2*
Get John to teach us all how to surf	*#3*
Join Deb's hockey team	*#4*
Go out with the girls or organise a girls' weekend away	*#5*
Have coffee dates	*#6*
Go to school assembly once a month	*#7*
Teach the kids how to play 500	
Start and finish some good books	
Go to the movies, on my own!	
Sleep	
Sort out my music list on the iPod	
Learn how to use my computer properly	
Stay at the hairdressers long enough to have my hair styled rather than just dried	
Get my eyebrows waxed to keep them in shape rather than when they get to the point of no return. Same for rest of body hair.	

Nice Work. Now You Know:

- What you want to Insource and what you want to Outsource
- You have set up your Insourcing List, obtained family buy-in, and actioned it - you have your kids and partner on the job
- You have set up your Outsourcing List, prioritised what tasks you will Outsource and you have started actioning it
- You have identified your Complete Rejects and the tasks you will now do a lot smarter, prioritised what tasks you will get rid of first, and you have started actioning it
- You have updated your Wants List, prioritised what you want to do first and you have started actioning it.

It's time to TAKE CONTROL.

STEP 5: TAKE CONTROL

Well done lady - you are about to take the controls! You have identified hours of quality time you can get back, and it's now time to turn the theory and exercises into tangible Actions to realise and sustain your big time savings.

Don't worry! You aren't being left to your own devices. I will work closely with you to help you maintain your momentum with consistency and persistency. Your mantra is *30 Extra Hours a Month!* Don't forget it.

You should be where Alice is. Let's see ...

◇◇

Alice's Me Time Diary

OK, this is where I'm at:

- *Insourcing List is done. Held a family meeting to discuss what else could be added to the List and the kids, somewhat reluctantly, agreed that it was probably a good idea that they chip in to help around the house. Not least because Mum is at her wit's end and might just spontaneously combust if help is not forthcoming.*

~ *I made three copies of the Insourcing List, laminated them to make them indestructible, and placed them strategically around the house (blue tacked to Henry's bedroom wall; blue tacked to Olive's bedroom wall; and in the bathroom - where most of the stuff seems to live in small self-sustaining communities.) Considered tacking one to John's head, but refrained when he openly declared what a good idea my Insourcing List was. Bless him.*

~ *I have shown John how to hang up his towel properly - poor man, seemed somewhat bewildered. More so, I have reminded him where the laundry is and demonstrated how the dirty clothes drawer next to the washing machine is very easy to pull out and deposit his dirty clothes in. Given it is only 5 or 6 steps from the bedroom floor to the laundry, I am confident he can make the journey each day without getting lost. So far, so good.*

~ *I am still struggling to turn a blind eye to the crap that lies around. I do catch myself picking it up and removing it. However, there have been an increasing number of occasions where I have just kicked the wet towels from my path, summoned all of my willpower, and walked on.*

~ *I have written up a list of general family chores and divided them up between the kids. Just this week I have added the nights John will cook (and the kids will clean up) and the nights I will cook (and the kids will clean up).*

~ *After much negotiation, I capitulated and agreed to pay the kids pocket money each week to do the general chores. I think this will help keep them motivated, plus they needed a bit of a win on this, the poor down-trodden little slave children.*

~ *I have had to remind the kids every single day to do their chores. Feel like a whinging old mole - am I yelling more than I was before I started this process? How much longer before it is no longer a chore for me to get the kids to do their chores? Need to hang in there. The one chore which is regularly working without a reminder is feeding the pets, so it is starting to work.*

~ *Hired a housekeeper. Yes I did! Life changing. Really. John and I did have one massive fight over the housekeeper because he only wanted her to come once a fortnight and I wanted her to come once a week. In the end we agreed to make it fortnightly on a trial basis.*

~ *Rejects done - they were actually easy to implement, so I virtually wiped them all out at once. What will be more challenging is making sure they don't creep back into my day - this is a WIP.*

~ *I have started meditation class. Ommm. Oh, and I have read a book.*

◇◇◇

Maintaining the momentum

Gyms stay in business for one reason, and one reason only - they have a lot of unmotivated members who initially joined up with very good intentions of regularly exercising, but who, over time, lost momentum and now rarely use their memberships. It is a business model built on having as many clients fail as possible. Look at it this way, if everyone who joined your local gym turned up day in and out ready to exercise, your local gym would go out of business. It would not have enough space, treadmills, bikes and weights to meet the demands of all of its eager beaver well-buffed clients.

As a successful business owner or career woman, you have not built your success banking on working with unmotivated clients. You have built your success by setting goals, driving hard to win and by staying motivated.

The same goes for transforming your time.

But, like a gym membership which rarely gets used, you might experience moments of procrastination and frustration when implementing the *5 Steps to Being SMART* and you might even want to give up. That's OK. It's how you respond to these moments that will mark you out. No-one said it would be easy. This book is not called *Me Time - The Professional Woman's Guide to finding 30 guilt-free hours by Complete and Utter Magic*. So, make a commitment, stay positive and set yourself up for success and not for failure.

We are going to build you an Action Plan - but you need to take ownership of this one.

It wouldn't be fun if it was easy

So, what could go wrong? There will be three big hurdles you may need to navigate:

1. You will be your own worst enemy.

- You need to invest time to make time. Carve out the time you need to implement your behavioural changes or else it just won't happen.
- When it comes to Insourcing, do not be tempted to just do it all yourself because: *it's easier; it will save a fight; you feel that you should; you really don't mind doing it; it only takes 5 minutes; it really is your job after all;* and so on and so on and so on. Stay strong. Never forget what doing the *small stuff* was costing you. If you start to lose your way, remember you were losing days of your life every year to the *small stuff*.
- If you find yourself falling into old habits like checking emails a thousand times a day or flicking in and out of Facebook, don't. Just don't. Stay strong - you are in control here.
- During the first 60 days much of what you used to do

but which you have promised yourself you will no longer do, will be lying around on the floor simply begging you to deal with it. Don't. Stay strong - you are in control here.

- Give yourself a break. One of the biggest time wasters is grappling with problems or trying to make decisions that you really need to leave alone because you don't have the answers right now. If this happens, park it and come back to it at a set time (e.g., revisit this at 2pm Friday.) By tucking the problem away, your subconscious will mull it over uninterrupted.

2. Ha! You thought you were your worst enemy. Wrong. Your kids will be your worst enemies.

- Your kids will not take these changes lying down (even though lying down often seems to be their preferred position when it comes to helping around the house). Your children will not be cheering you on from the side lines in your campaign to manage your time the SMART way. On the contrary they will be actively working against you. The Insourcing changes you make will not be popular with them, because it means more work for them. They have suddenly been evicted from the executive floor of the hotel and they will be shocked and annoyed at having lost access to their personal Maid service (a.k.a. You).
- Your kids are not stupid - they will try every trick in the book in an attempt to wear you down. They will whinge, complain, argue and talk back. They will compliment you as being better at this stuff than them. They will explain that they are too busy to do any chores because you told them they had to do their homework. They will tell you they have done their chores when they have not. They will disappear. The list of their devious behaviour

is seemingly endless. It's your turn to prove that you are not stupid. Stay strong.

- Your kids may well pretend they don't know how to do something. Don't believe them. Besides, you now have another weapon in your arsenal - data. You now know exactly how long it takes you to do a task, which you can share with your kids. Try something like, *'Making your bed will only take you 1 minute. I know because I timed it. Yes, that is weird, but that's beside the point. Let me show you how to make your bed. Now let me mess it up and you try. It's all yours! The more often you do it, the faster you will get.'*

— *What other women say* —

Fatima Dib, Business Owner, Smart Financial Solutions

I'm a single mum with four children. When my kids used to leave their things lying around I would ask, and ask, and ask them to clean up. Then eventually I would get frustrated and say, 'It's easier if I do it myself'. I stopped saying that when my kids took my words and used them against me - 'But Mum, it's easier if you just do it yourself.' Not anymore!

3. ***And then there is your partner.***

- It is also quite possible that your partner will not take these changes lying down. To take the pressure off yourself, you need to discuss with your partner the changes you want to make and, more importantly, how you as an individual, how you as a couple, and how you as a family, will benefit from the new arrangements.

- Implementing and benefitting from the changes you make, as a family, will be much easier if you have your partner's buy-in. Get your partner to read *Me Time* - they might learn something!

One day at a time

The key to staying the course is Commitment, Repetition, Consistency and Recalibration.

> ***— What other women say —***
>
> Megan Dalla-Camina, Strategist and Author
>
> *You need to constantly recalibrate to ensure you have the right priorities in place. It never ends. You can never become complacent.*

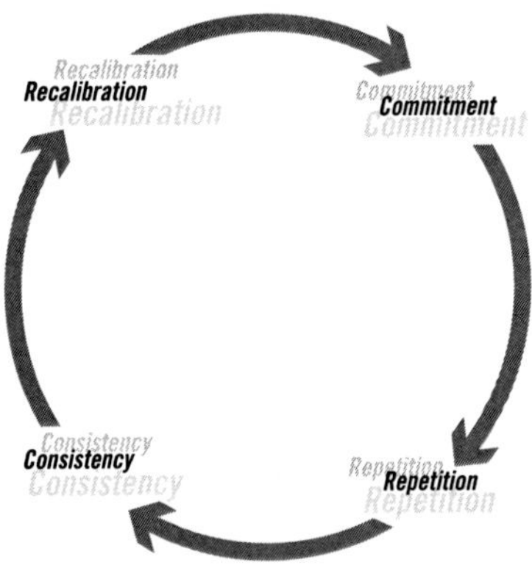

> ***Commitment***
>
> You know you want to get back 30 hours a month. You know this won't happen by magic. If you want it you need to work for it. Every time you feel yourself losing a little momentum, let your gaze linger fondly on your *Commitment Certificate* and focus on the gain: you will get back 30 hours a month if you commit to doing so. In fact, you have already identified where those hours are going to come from - now all you need to do is act.

Repetition

The more you repeat your new habits (and the more you stop repeating your crazy old habits), the more ingrained your new behaviours will become. We all know this stuff. It's not a theory that is about to win me the Pulitzer. Perfect practice makes perfect. Keep your eye on the prize. And again, repetition means repeating your own new behaviours, and regularly reminding your family to repeat their new behaviours.

Consistency

It's important to be consistent. Not just for your own wee tired brain, but for those around you who you are trying to re-program.

For example, if you explain to your son that from now on he must make his own bed before you will take him to footy training, you need to be consistent. If you enforce the rule twice and then the next time you let the rule slide because he is running late for training, you are sending your son mixed messages. And, like any kid with an ounce of spunk, when you next try to enforce the rule, your son will (rightly) respond along the lines of: *'But muuuuuum, you let me go to training last time without making my bed! Can't I just do it later*?'*

** Your son's definition of Later = Never. Because now he knows that he has you on the ropes, he will leave his bed unmade for so long that eventually you will give up and do it yourself OR his sheets may well grow legs and walk to the laundry.*

Recalibration

Continue to revisit your Musts, Wants, Delegates and Rejects because as you gain momentum you will realise there are more changes to make and more hours to reclaim. You will also need to recalibrate as your priorities or life circumstances change.

Action time!

You *can* install new habits. You *can* sustain the changes you have made. And, what's more, you will become so good at managing your Musts, Delegates and Rejects that you will get back additional time to do more of what you love - the Wants.

What you need is an Action Plan, or timetable. To successfully implement and then sustain your changes, your Action Plan must be realistic and achievable. Don't put so many changes into the first few days that you set yourself up for failure. Big mistake.

At a high level, you will go through three phases over the next 90 days:

30 Days	Content Focus The first 30 days will be a period of content focus. You are motivated and committed to changing. This stuff is easy! It's exciting as you start to complete the exercises and some of the actions, and you can see that there are hours of lost time up for grabs. Keep going!
60 Days	Implementation The next 30 days will be a period of implementation, where you turn the theory in your exercises into practice. This may test your resolve - you may be tempted to slip back into your old ways because it may feel the simpler road. Plus, you are fighting the battle on two fronts: against yourself and against your family. Stay strong!
90 Days	Maintain The next 30 days will be rewarding as your new habits, and your new family habits, become more ingrained. It's working, now keep it up!

Exercise - Action it Baby!

Purpose

To set up your Action Plan, ensuring you implement the changes you have identified and that you maintain your momentum over 90 days and beyond.

Get out the Action Plan template from the *Me Time* Workbook. There is an extract of the Action Plan below - Alice uses column 'Actions' to include her self-talk commentary, but you only need to make a list of Actions.

Use your preferred Tools (for example, your Daily Planner) from Part 3, *Me Time* Tops Tools, to schedule time in 30 days (i.e.: from day 60) to revisit your Action Plan and update the Status Column. Do this again in a further 30 days (i.e.: from day 90).

Feel free to email me with a copy of your Action Plan on Day 1 as soon as you have drafted it. I will review it and then contact you direct. How motivating is that!?

PHASE	ACTION ITEM	ACTIONS	Status
30 Days: Content Focus	Accountability		
	Me Time Workbook, exercises and actions		
	Motivation		

	Scheduling		
	Insourcing		
	Outsourcing		
	Rejects		
	Wants		
60 Days: Implementation	Musts, Wants, Delegates and Rejects		
90 Days: Maintain	Musts, Wants, Delegates and Rejects		

Alice's Me Time Diary

Here are my actions for the full 90 days. Plus now that I am on my way, I have started marking up my Status Column.

PHASE	ACTION ITEM	ACTIONS	Status
30 Days: Content Focus	Accountability	*There is nothing better than group accountability - no backing out from that. I know my friends will be interested that I have taken on this time transformation challenge. They will encourage and congratulate me. But most importantly, they will keep me accountable. But if they laugh and jeer at me, well that will only spur me on!* *Nothing like a little healthy peer group pressure.* *I will post this today on Facebook (at a designated time!): 'Guess what? I am reading Me Time and I'm going to get back 30 hours a month of 'Me Time' to live the life I want! The first thing I am going to do with my extra time is take a class in how to meditate. Ommm.'*	*Done*
	Me Time Workbook, exercises and actions	*On Monday 1st I will print out the Me Time Workbook.* *Over the next 30 days I will complete all exercises and actions.*	*Done* *Done. Yay!*
	Motivation	*If I waiver I will visualise my Wants.* *If I waiver I will remember the benefits: 30 hours a month, 30 hours a month, repeat. Ommm.* *I will keep a Journal of this time transformation journey to keep a track of my progress. That will definitely help with motivation!*	*WIP* *WIP* *Done, and WIP*
	Scheduling	*I will use my Tools (Part 3, Me Time Tools) to lock in the time I need to deal with all actions associated with my Musts, Wants, Delegates and Rejects.* *I already have a Family Planner, but I am going to get a Monthly and a Daily Planner. These will be my new bibles and I absolutely commit to opening and filling them in every day until it becomes second nature.* *I will sit down with the family on a Sunday night to fill in the Family Planner with our commitments.*	*Done and WIP* *Mostly doing this. Need to get better.* *Done and working well*
	Insourcing	*On Monday 15th I will draft my Insourcing List and then sit down with the kids and John to brainstorm what else can be added. Getting them involved will help with family buy-in. I will explain why, as a family, we are going to Insource and I will get everyone to agree that Family is a Team Sport. Yay Team – let's get Mum her life back!*	*Done*

		I will make sure everyone is clear on what they are responsible for and what will happen if they lapse . . .	*Done*
		I will put copies of the Insourcing List in Henry's and Olive's rooms and on the fridge. *If this fails, I will buy a big white board, write out the Insourcing List, and place it in front of the TV.*	*Done*
		If I see my family's stuff lying around just begging me to pick it up I will take a deep breath and leave it on the floor. This is going to kill me.	*Hard. I am doing this, mostly*
		I will embrace my inner-harpy. I will regularly remind my family of what they agreed to do.	*Done again and again*
		I have decided to pay the kids pocket money for the general chores - we all need to be rewarded for making change.	*Done*
		I will make sure we celebrate the successes - a special family dinner or a trip to the movies.	*Done and WIP*
		Maintain Journal	*Ongoing*
	Outsourcing	*On Tuesday 16th I will make a copy of my Outsourcing List and stick it next to my computer.*	*Done*
		From the items I have ticked, I will choose one task to outsource ASAP (housekeeper!), and will have locked in my housekeeper by the 30th.	*Done!!*
		I will Outsource to get some help with the kids - a Mothers' Helper - within two weeks and lock that in by the 14th of next month.	*Done*
		I will try and get John to Outsource the gardening - lock that in by the 31st of next month.	*Done*
		I will keep working through my Outsourcing List to see what else I can Outsource.	*WIP*
		Maintain Journal	*Ongoing*
	Rejects	*On Wednesday 17thI will make a copy of my Rejects List and stick it on the fridge and next to my computer.*	*Done*
		Need to sort out the whole supermarket disaster first. No more trips to the supermarket at lunchtime. No more daily trips on the way home. Try for once a week proper shop - reject from the 17th.	*Done*
		Then work through the rest of my Rejects list.	*WIP*
		I will revisit my Rejects regularly and make sure they are still Rejected.	*Not done*
		I will workshop with the girls to see if there are other tasks I can Reject.	
		Maintain Journal	*Ongoing*

Continued ...

... continued

	Wants	*I will update my original Wants List, prioritise my Wants and put the list in my Daily Planner on Saturday 20th.* *I will choose and schedule time for one new Want every single week starting from Monday 22nd! My biggest Want is to learn meditation. Plus I want to see more of the girls, date nights with John, family surf safari.* *The list of Wants is huge! I plan to mix this up so I can get a sense of what I enjoy most.* *Maintain Journal*	*Done* *WIP* *Ongoing*
60 Days: Implmentation	Wants, Musts, Delegates and Rejects	*I will reward myself (and my family) for each success.* *I will take note of what is working well, and think about why and try and leverage this.* *I will take note of what isn't working and come up with a better solution.* *When I feel unmotivated I will read my Journal to see how far I have come, paying special attention to how spending time on my Wants makes me feel.*	
90 Days: Maintain		*I will have addressed all of my Rejects.* *Insourcing to be tracking well. My kids will be getting on top of their chores, but if not, a regular reminder is not going to kill them. I may have to harp from time to time, but less so.* *I will have addressed my top 3 Outsourcing tasks. My domestic helpers will have started, will be on track and I will be completely in love with them.*	
		I will be seeing hours of time coming back into my month, and I will schedule this reclaimed time into my Daily Planner for my Wants. *I will be using my new Tools every day and this will be a habit.* *I am not losing momentum, because this stuff has worked!* *Month 4 - I will schedule some time to revisit my new Standard Day to see if I am making the best use of my time - there might be other tasks I can Reject, Insource or Outsource.*	

This is so empowering. Yes it is! Action List completed (see above). The first task I outsourced was Housekeeping - I actually killed a few birds with one stone, as the housekeeper tidies, cleans, irons, and does some food prep for dinner! Why on earth did I not do this earlier? After a while John fell on his sword and agreed weekly is better than fortnightly - the weeks the housekeeper has been are like living at a resort, while the intervening weeks started to see the house descend back into grunge city. Big win for Mama! It's blissful no longer having to clean the shower screen and scrape the grout between the tiles. Plus, now the toilets are cleaned every single week as opposed to whenever I remember (which to be honest was not often enough).

Then I found a Mother's Helper. Bless her. Jilly started 3 weeks ago and already she has changed my life. I no longer have to rush home from the city during peak hour to collect the kids every day. Jilly runs the kids to all of their afterschool activities (Olive finally has an enthralled audience for her dance lesson), drives the kids home and sets them up doing their homework, and helps them too. She has them unpack their school bags, clean out their lunch boxes and then she gets them started on their rooms! My God.

John was a reluctant convert, but eventually agreed to give a gardener a go - hired this month. The gardener has been once and did the edges, around every tree, and blew the leaves away with his blowy machine thing, and he was so quick. After one visit John is sold on this and has put his mower and whipper snipper on eBay. He tells me he plans to use the money to buy a surfboard so that he can teach the kids to surf. Now that I would pay to watch!

We haven't planned the surf trip as yet because it is too damned cold, but we did a family trip to this enormous Surf City complex and bought wetsuits for all. Look absolutely ridiculous, but can't wait to hit the waves (I even sound like a surfy chick).

I have found time!

So far this month John and I have had one date night every single week. We have tried a few new restaurants and just used one night to go for a walk together. Simple, but nice.

Eyebrows waxed: tick. Nether region waxed: tick. Date night here I come!

We are starting to get back the time, energy and head space to interact like a proper family. It's good.

◇◇

Question time

You are bound to have questions - the most common of which are set out below. If you have other questions, find your answers at www.timestylers.com.au.

I am lacking motivation, what can I do?	If you are starting to waiver, there is a lot you can do to get back on track: Compare your Standard Day to your Dream Day Revisit your Values and their priorities Remind yourself that you are not a slave Look at your list of Wants Remember why you bought *Me Time* in the first place When you catch yourself falling into an old bad time habit, write it down on a piece of paper and stick it next to your computer as a reminder of what you don't want to do: STOP PROCRASTINATING. Often a visual reminder is enough to keep you on track.
I've done the *5 Steps to Being SMART*, am I finished?	Get into the habit of revisiting your lists of Musts, Wants, Delegates, and Rejects each month. These lists will change depending on what is happening in your life at the time. As you recalibrate your Musts, Wants, Delegates and Rejects ask yourself, 'Is this the best use of my time?'

I have lots of time back, where to now?	If you are using some of your 30 hours to spend more time on growing your business or successful career, now is a good time to revisit your Delegates. If you are earning more money and want to continue to do so then consider outsourcing more of the tasks you don't want or need to do yourself. For example: Engage someone to do the shopping for you. Get that same person to put the shopping away, organise your pantry and fridge, set up a meal plan and cook the meals. Engage a housekeeper to manage your home. They can help keep your house tidy, do the laundry, change the bed linen, vacuum the floors, collect the dry cleaning, run the errands, pay the bills and coordinate your kids' afterschool activities. Engage a handyman to come once a month to mow the lawns, wash the windows, and do any odd jobs that need doing. Engage a regular babysitter so that you can have a weekly date night with your partner. Engage an 'organiser' to wait at your home for the technician who has given you a 5-hour window for when he will turn up to install your new telephone system. While the organiser is waiting, have them re-organise your wardrobe and your linen cupboard.
Can I really have it all?	Remind yourself that having it all really means having the bits you want. And then remind yourself that having the bits you want doesn't mean that you are responsible for doing it all on your own.

Nice Work. Now You Know:

- Some of the pitfalls and the excuses your family will try and use against you from time to time. You may well have thought up a few more. As they say, forewarned is forearmed
- How to maintain your momentum
- How to set up your Action Plan and implement it
- Like every Step in the *5 Steps to Being SMART*, Step 5 Take Control will only work if you make it work.

It's time for your Tools.

PART 3

ME TIME TOP TOOLS

ME TIME TOP TOOLS

In managing your time the SMART way, and maximising the use of your time, you need a suite of great Tools - Tools which help you plan and protect your time.

As a successful professional or business woman, you will undoubtedly already use many of the Tools below to help manage your busy work and equally busy home life. Part Three will show you how you can now use these Tools in the context of finding 30 plus hours every month.

There are dozens of different time management Tools to choose from - you can use them as paper-based Tools; you can use Tools on your computer; or there are plenty of time management Apps available for your smartphone. If you want online tools and Apps, then just google what's available as new online tools and Apps are coming up all the time. They all do exactly the same thing as the paper base tools, so go with what you are most comfortable with and which you are most likely to use properly. One word of warning - if you use a combination of online and offline Tools, make sure you coordinate them to ensure they are in sync.

The key is to select Tools which:

- are right for you (if you are a bit of a technophobe, then you are probably better off selecting offline Tools)
- you can keep with you and use on the go
- you will enjoy using
- help facilitate the management of your time, as opposed to Tools which are so cumbersome that they are actually a waste of your time.

Me Time Top Tools

The beauty of the *Me Time* Top Tools is that they can be used to build on each other, getting you from A to B; for example, if you like to start with a Daily To Do List, you can use that to inform your Weekly, Monthly and Annual Planners. Alternatively, you might like to start with your Annual Plan and work backwards by breaking tasks down into Monthly, Weekly and Daily tasks so getting you from B to A.

Annual Planner

Annual Planners are excellent for blocking out major projects months in advance. With the effective use of an Annual Planner, there is no way you will risk turning down a once-in-a-lifetime opportunity because you think it might be on at the same time as your family holiday.

Use your Annual Planner to block out your Musts, including things like school holidays, annual leave, family holidays, conferences for work which might conflict with home activities, school sports carnivals, and birthdays. Also show work events for your partner, where he/she might be away for several days or weeks.

Annual Planners are also the perfect first step if you like setting annual family or annual business goals.

What to do:

1. Work out whether you prefer to work with a calendar year format or a financial year format, and then buy your Annual Planner 4-6 weeks before the end of the year
2. Update your Annual Planner as new significant Musts arise
3. Cross reference your Annual Planner with your Monthly/Weekly/Daily Planners each month to ensure consistency
4. Check out the Time Stylers Annual Planner at www.timestylers.com.au

— What other women say —

Nicola Moras, Kickass Marketing Mentor

At the start of the year I sit down and write my business goals for the year ahead. Then I break these down into 90-day blocks; then tasks to be completed in each 30 day block; then into a weekly To Do List, and then a daily To Do list.

If I achieve all of my weekly goals then I have a great chance of achieving my monthly goals, and so on. Reverse-engineering works for me. It takes me a couple of hours to set this out at the start of the year. And then once a week, generally a Sunday night, I sit down and recalibrate the week ahead. This only takes me 10 minutes.

This system has saved my butt so many times!

Monthly Planner

Monthly Planners have a page for each month of the year. They allow you see your month at a glance, and what time you have committed. Monthly Planners are excellent for planning events in advance (birthdays, appointments) and for tracking repeat activities (kids' basketball games, after-school activities, date night). By blocking out this time and planning ahead, you won't double book or over-book any given time.

Monthly Planners are also very useful for breaking down your annual business or family goals (taken from your Annual Planner), allowing you to rearrange and manage your time flexibly to cater for any unforeseen or unexpected work and life events.
What to do:

1. As with all time management Tools, select the Monthly Planner which works best for your circumstances. For example, if you have four kids as well as a busy career or business, go for a Monthly Planner with space for every family member
2. Update your Monthly Planner as new significant Musts arise
3. Schedule time in your Monthly Planner for your Wants
4. Schedule time in your Monthly Planner to deal with your Delegates
5. Cross reference your Monthly Planner with your Annual/Weekly/Daily Planners each month to ensure consistency
6. Check out the Time Stylers Monthly Planner at www.timestylers.com.au

Weekly Planner

Your Weekly Planner is perfect for scheduling what each member of your family has planned each week, giving you a complete and easy-to-track overview of the week ahead. By scheduling effectively, you will avoid catastrophes such as forgotten birthday parties.

Use your Weekly Planner to manage both your home and work commitments. For example, by including the dates and time of your work Musts as well as the dates and time of your Home Musts (such as when you are responsible for the kids' car pool pick-up and drop-off), will mean that you do not double book, or worse, forget a commitment you have made.

When your first child starts school, time management can go out the window. And, as parents, we are entirely to blame for this. We have created these crazy little social animals who we enrol in every conceivable opportunity that comes their way.

This is our fault. Sometime you just have to say No to your children (revisit *Sorry it's a No from me* on page 12.). But assuming that at this point in time you do not want to break little Eric's heart by not letting him try out for the Under 6-Year-old Irish Dancing Representative Team, then what you need as a matter of urgency lady, is a really good Weekly Planner. This is especially so if you have more than one child.

From about the age of 5, if not before, if you have particularly talented offspring, your kids will be doing everything from school excursions, sports days, music lessons, after-school sport/music/dancing/acting/cooking/singing/painting/pottery/French, special school assemblies, school/sport/music/holiday camps, birthday parties, prep graduation ceremonies and the occasional spacewalk with NASA.

If you don't write these events down (multiplied by the number of kids you have) then frankly you will be screwed. Take this advice from someone who did not write down her daughter's best friend's 3-year-old fairy birthday party 7 years ago: the wound is still fresh.

What to do:

1. Update your Weekly Planner as new Musts arise
2. Review your Weekly Planner each Sunday night and make sure everyone knows what they have scheduled for the week ahead
3. Lock in time to set up your Delegates and to enjoy your Wants
4. Cross-reference your Weekly Planner with your Annual/Monthly/Daily Planner each month to ensure consistency
5. Keep your Weekly Planner in the kitchen and train everyone on how to read it and how to use it
6. Check out the Time Stylers Weekly Planner at www.timestylers.com.au

— *What other women say* —

Holly Kramer, CEO Best & Less

I sit down once a week and forward plan my Weekly diary for the next 8-10 weeks. I note all the key things I have on - eg. a birthday, and then I work backwards a week or so to remind myself that I have to buy a gift for the birthday the following week. That's how I keep on top of everything.

Carolyn Creswell, Founder Carman's

Be conscious of what you say yes to. Your kids don't need to go to every single party they are invited to. Just because you are 'free' on the weekend does not mean it is convenient. Make a decision on the invite and respond straight away - that way you only think about the decision once and not 5 times.

Daily Planner

With one page to a day, there is plenty of room in a Daily Planner to record all of your appointments and any notes - keeping all the important stuff in one place.

What to do:

1. You need to open it, use it, and review it every single day
2. Update your Daily Planner as every new appointment arises - this is the bible for recording your daily Musts
3. Lock in time to set up your Delegates and to enjoy your Wants
4. Cross-reference your Daily Planner with your Annual/ Monthly/Weekly Planner each month to ensure consistency
5. Ensure your Daily Planner is the right size to allow you to easily take it with you wherever you go - something you can slip into your bag or laptop case
6. Check out the Time Stylers Daily Planner at www.timestylers.com.au

Daily To Do List

Your To Do List is the Gold Nugget of time management Tools. Planning your To Dos for the following day, every day, before going to bed will allow you to park your mental list on paper and then sleep well, knowing you have a plan for tackling tomorrow.

What to do:

1. Every night think about the time you have available the following day. Do this in conjunction with your Daily and/or Weekly Planner
2. Note down your essential/urgent Must tasks first (e.g., Monday meeting at 9am with Accountant; meeting 11am with team, and so on)
3. Next identify and prioritise other Musts. Where possible, prioritise these in an order which is consistent with your Values
4. Make and record a realistic assessment of the time each Must will take. It's important that you allocate appropriate blocks of time, or else your day will be thrown out and you will find yourself playing catch-up. Learn as you go - if you allocate 20 minutes to a typical task but it regularly takes you 30 minutes, then adjust
5. Be prepared to be flexible because not all days will run smoothly. Factor in the possibility that you may need to dedicate time to something unpredictable (like when the school calls to tell you your daughter needs stitches ...)
6. Put a big cross through every task you complete on your To Do list, because it looks great and it will keep you motivated
7. Use your To Do List to lock in time to set up your Delegates and enjoy your Wants

8. Give yourself a break every hour or so. Get up, stretch, breathe, make a cup of tea and reflect on your completed To Do List items with real satisfaction. Go girl!
9. Check out the Time Stylers Daily To Do Lists at www.timestylers.com.au

— *What other women say* —

Janine Allis, Founder and Managing Director Boost Juice (Retail Zoo)

During your journey you might feel overwhelmed. But when you write a list you will realise that it's under control. I love lists and I love the endorphins when you cross something off your list! Nothing will be forgotten if you have a list.

Amy Poynton, Business Advisor, Board Member (retired partner Ernst & Young)

My best piece of advice is to spend 20 minutes at the end of each day planning for the next day. I list what I have accomplished and then I plan for the next day. It's highly effective.

On a Sunday night, when I am relaxed and in the right frame of mind, I plan for the week ahead. 20 minutes tops.

Christie Nicholas, Director, Kids Business Communications

Every day I identify my Big 3 meatiest priorities that must be completed by the end of the day. Then there are lots of little 'filler' tasks - but I always do the Big 3 first. I select the Big 3 by asking myself 'What are the most beneficial tasks for my business today?'

Megan Dalla-Camina, Strategist and Author

If I had to choose just one productivity tool it would be my daily To Do List. I find that using pen and paper is the most efficient way for me to work. It gets everything out of my head and it helps me manage my energy, my passion, my business and my life.

Weekly Meal Planner

A Weekly Meal Planner serves one purpose and one purpose only - it saves you significant amounts of time you would otherwise spend each day (i) standing in front of the fridge thinking about what to cook for dinner, and (ii) going to the supermarket because you don't have all of the ingredients you need.

What to do:

1. This one is a Family tool. Once a week get everyone to come up with a couple of meal ideas. Even better, get each person to nominate the meal they are going to make for the family
2. Fill out the Weekly Meal Planner, identifying what is on the menu and who is the cook
3. For each meal, check the fridge, freezer and pantry to make sure you have all the ingredients you need
4. Any ingredient you don't have should be written on your Weekly Shopping List
5. Check out the Time Stylers Weekly Meal Planner at www.timestylers.com.au

Weekly Shopping List

Your Weekly Shopping List will save you going to the supermarket every single day. Simple.

What to do:

1. Working with your Weekly Meal Plan, write down the ingredients you don't have
2. Check the pantry, fridge, freezer, bathrooms and laundry to see if you have the family staples (milk, bread, toilet paper, washing powder, pet food), and ask everyone in the family whether there is anything they think the household needs. Once your kids are old enough to make their own breakfast, they can also be taught to let you know when a pantry or fridge item is down to the last one. As they get a bit older, then can actually add the item to the shopping list
3. If you have storage room, stock up on non-perishables every few months
4. Check out the Time Stylers Weekly Shopping List at www.timestylers.com.au

Insourcing List

Your Insourcing List will sit somewhere very prominent in your home so that everyone (children and partner) know what tasks they are responsible for on a daily basis. Like Alice, you will love your Insourcing List, your kids less so.

What to do:

1. Go back to Step 4 Reframe to refresh yourself on:
   - why you need to Insource
   - what you said you would Insource
   - what Alice chose to Insource.
2. With your Action Plan (Step 5 Take Control), schedule time into your preferred Planner to sit down with your family and identify:
   - every task you want each child to be responsible for
   - every task you want your partner to be responsible for

- the tasks that can be rotated between family members each week.

3. Write it up, explain it to everyone, and don't budge from it
4. Put it somewhere obvious, where everyone can see it
5. Each time someone forgets to do one of their tasks, remind them. Be consistent.

Outsourcing List

Your Outsourcing List will sit next to your computer as a reminder of what you want to Outsource.

What to do:

1. Go back to Step 4 Reframe to refresh yourself on:
   - why you need to Outsource
   - what you said you would Outsource
   - what Alice chose to Outsource.
2. Identify every task you want to Outsource
3. With your Action Plan (Step 5 Take Control), schedule time into your preferred Planner to contact the domestic helpers you want to engage, arrange a time to meet, select your preferred candidates, and away you go.

Nice Work. Now You Know:

- Not all of the above Tools will work for you - they are simply a selection of Tools which work very well when it comes to managing time.
- Decide what works best for you and make it happen.

It's your time now.

PART 4

WHERE TO NOW?

Thank you for reading Me Time.

Just in case you missed it, Step 5 Take Control was all about converting everything you have planned for in the *Me Time* Workbook into a real life Action Plan. Yes, it's over to you. All the best and enjoy each and every one of those hours you get back!

◇◇

Alice's Me Time Diary

A final word from Alice, 90 Days on

Without question I have more time. I have more than 30 hours back a month to do what I love. I am spending some of this time doing more work, some on myself and lots of quality time with my family. Olive and Henry can see the difference - I overheard them talking about me and Olive actually said 'Mum is fun!' Happy - I've always wanted to be fun.

I definitely feel a lot less guilt when I head off to work, knowing that tonight when I get home (to a clean house courtesy of our housekeeper, and a meal cooked by John) that I can sit with the kids and help with their homework rather than rush out to the supermarket, run the vacuum over the floor, clean the toilets and make the dinner.

And I feel no guilt at all when I sit down to family time.

On the down side, I still have to keep on top of the kids and their chores. I can't tell you how tempting it is just to clean up their stuff myself. But, I am staying strong! Yelling a bit, but they are starting to get the message. John, on the other hand, is transformed in his ability to put his dirty clothes in the wash - my threats to not wash anything that wasn't put in the laundry did the trick.

We have a housekeeper, a mother's helper, a guy who mows the lawn and it has changed my life and our family life.

My biggest challenge is staying on top of the Rejects list. I thought this would be the easy bit! It's very tempting to fall into the habit of hitting the supermarket every day, so I had to compromise and go twice a week.

We do one big shop a week, and then either John, the nanny or I do a second run for extra milk, bread and other stuff we need. It's not a total Reject outcome, but it's better than what it was and it is working for us.

I still felt a bit guilty about not going to Olive's dance class. But get this: having seen me plan out my time the SMART way, Olive wanted to map her own Values. And she identified 'dance' as something she was losing interest in, with a possible preference for - wait for it -soccer! I swear to God I had nothing to do with pointing out to her that we are more of a 'sporty family' than a 'dancing family'. Truly. I love soccer.

We have had two trips down the coast to 'surf' (if that's what you can call it.) The kids were unbelievable, both pretty much standing up and catching a wave straight away. Little buggers. Must be something about having a lower centre of gravity. I was bloody hopeless, which John and the kids LOVED - look at how hopeless Mum is! But when I finally stood up for about 30 seconds - they were delirious with joy. I haven't laughed so much for ages - so much so I wet myself - which happily kept the wet suit nice and warm. Yuk.

Date night continues. I am simply hair free in all the right places. I haven't joined the hockey team as yet, but have locked in a girls' weekend away - unbelievable.

But, it's now 'Me Time' according to my To Do List, so I'm off for a run.

I am Alice and I have transformed my time.

◇◇

First Aid Kit

Some readers will find a book requiring self-reflection to be valuable, but difficult to do in isolation. If you are such a person, there are a few avenues for you to consider:

1. Collaborate: work with a friend or a group to complete the *5 Steps to Being SMART*. Two plus heads are often better than one.

2. Although you are being encouraged to be self-sufficient, some readers will still prefer a personal guiding hand. Drop an email to info@timestylers.com.au with your contact details and we can discuss some coaching options with you.
3. For direct help finding skilled domestic helpers or help around your office, drop us a brief email to helpers@ timestylers.com.au and we will contact you.

ABOUT KATE

44 years old, 3 kids, clever, hard-working and holder of many roles, some guilt and moments of stress.

There was a time when there was a lot more guilt, stress and plenty of insomnia. Kate had three children in three and a half years which involved a lot of nappies and vomit (some of it hers) and sleepless nights, all while trying to maintain her career and run a home. Kate worked part time, full time, from home, in the office, on her days off and occasionally from the crèche (she would leave work and drive home at lunchtime to breast feed baby number 2 … yep). Later, as Kate's kids started Kindergarten and school she was that mum who turned up looking a million dollars in her cute little twin set and high heels and tried to deposit the child who was clinging to her leg with tears in his eyes without getting too much snot on her lovely skirt, all while desperately trying to flee back to the car with her child's wails in one ear and her phone at the other dialling into a conference call, with half her mind on whether her son was still crying and what did those other mothers think of her?

Oh yes, she was living the dream.

Something had to give. Eventually it was Kate. She left her executive job and stayed at home with her kids. And what that time out gave her was the head space to REFRAME. To realise that there had to be a better way for other successful female professionals, who also happened to be mums or planned to be mums, to find hours of lost time, to lose their guilt and their stress, and have success on both the work and the home front.

Kate decided to focus her energy into what she cares about most - helping busy successful women understand that having it all does not mean doing it all.

Me Time is Kate's first book. With lots of information out there on time management Kate wanted to write something unique, practical, and easy to read and implement.

Kate blogs at www.timestylers.com.au, jump online to subscribe. Kate is also a professional speaker. If you would like to book Kate to speak to the very clever female employees in your company or to your networking group, contact her directly at info@timestylers.com.au.

CONTACTING TIME STYLERS

Kate is the Managing Director of Time Stylers and co-founder of Babysitters and More (BaM). Kate devotes her time to working with very busy, successful female professionals and business owners to help them manage their time the SMART way. The team at Time Stylers have a reputation for getting their clients back 30 hours a month to live the life they want. The Time Stylers approach is to combine coaching, education and access to fantastic domestic support to identify and sustain a much smarter personal time management system to free up hours of your precious time.

Time Stylers resources and training programs include:

- **Free videos:** get some great ideas and motivation for managing your time smarter
- **eBooks:** delve deeper into the *5 Steps to Being SMART* and tap into a supply of time saving power tips
- **Babysitters and More:** the Time Stylers outsourcing portal

- **Time Transformation Programs:** each designed to maximise the number of hours you get back each month
- **Personalised Time Transformation:** by application only, and includes Kate Christie for personal coaching.

Contact Time Stylers at
info@timestylers.com.au

TESTIMONIALS FOR TIME TRANSFORMATION PROGRAMS

The illusion that I would find more time 'when the kids are older' was recently shattered - I learned that it is not about external forces changing…it is about me learning how to find and manage 'Me Time'. The 5 Steps to being SMART gave me the insights and tools to choose how to spend my time so I can embrace and enjoy all the joys of life.

- Amy

~

I didn't expect to find any spare time with the 5 Steps to Being SMART. *I'm a busy person and my attitude was, 'Sorry, not a lot of time wasted through the week. I am always doing two things at once.' After completing the* 5 Steps to Being SMART *I identified an hour and a half a day of time I could get back. I was surprised and delighted.*

- Fiona

~

I've worked through the steps [of the 5 Steps to Being SMART]. I have started reviewing what I'm actually doing in my week and realised I can definitely get back time. I've delegated more to my children and even outsourced to get some balance at home with the family. Thanks for shifting my focus on how I can get more quality time with the family and for myself!

- Rachael

~

Working through the [5 Steps to Being SMART] is very thought-provoking and certainly heightens awareness around the value of your time. It also drives a reality check on how you are spending your time together with an opportunity to consider your distribution of effort across the things in your life that matter the most.

- Sue

~

I didn't have enough time for myself and to explore my interests, particularly as a single mother. The 5 Steps to Being SMART helped me find 4 hours a day I could reclaim by managing my time smarter. Now I just have to implement it and sustain it. I have also decided to spend some time on myself.

- Fatima

~

I do feel guilty about not spending enough time with my children. They are only this age once and I want them to remember me as being there for them during the important years. I am an efficient person and yet I found hours a day that I could use by managing my time smarter. Tidying and cleaning the house, being a taxi driver and email management are the areas I still need to work on. I hadn't thought about outsourcing some of these tasks!

- Sarah

My career is currently on hold as I have three children and I am essentially a single mum for six months of the year while my husband works interstate. With more time, eventually I would love to return to study. With the 5 Steps to Being SMART, Insourcing was my biggest realisation. This will save me 1.5 hours a day.

- Phoebe

~

After working through the 5 Steps to Being SMART I managed to identify an additional 3.5 hours a day of things I could delegate. For example, I took my kids into the bathroom the other day and showed them how to hang up their towels properly so they dry.

I love the practicality of the 5 Steps to Being SMART.

- Sarah

How about a Bonus?

If you have enjoyed *Me Time* and feel it deserves a 4- or 5-star review, please do so and send me a screenshot of your review at info@timestylers.com.au and I will send you some bonus content to say thank you.

If you found the content wanting, please email me your suggestions for inclusion in the 2nd edition.

Thanks!

Kate x